Repeated Financial Decisions

Repeated Financial Decisions: An Experimental Analysis

A Research Monograph

DARREN DUXBURY AND KEVIN KEASEY

JOHN WILEY & SONS, LTD
Chichester · New York · Weinheim · Brisbane · Singapore · Toronto

Copyright © 1999 by   John Wiley & Sons Ltd,
Baffins Lane, Chichester,
West Sussex PO19 1UD, England

National   01243 779777
International   (+44) 1243 779777
e-mail (for orders and customer service enquiries): cs-books@wiley.co.uk
Visit our Home Page on http://www.wiley.co.uk
or http://www.wiley.com

Other Wiley Editorial Offices

John Wiley & Sons, Inc., 605 Third Avenue,
New York, NY 10158-0012, USA

WILEY-VCH Verlag GmbH, Pappelallee 3,
D-69469 Weinheim, Germany

Jacaranda Wiley Ltd, 33 Park Road, Milton,
Queensland 4064, Australia

John Wiley & Sons (Asia) Pte Ltd, 2 Clementi Loop #02-01,
Jin Xing Distripark, Singapore 129809

John Wiley & Sons (Canada) Ltd, 22 Worcester Road,
Rexdale, Ontario M9W 1L1, Canada

Library of Congress Cataloging-in-Publication Data
Duxbury, Darren.
    Repeated financial decisions :   and experimental analysis : a
research monograph / Darren Duxbury and Kevin Keasey.
        p.   cm.
    Includes bibliographical references.
    ISBN 0-471-72028-3 (alk. paper)
    1. Stocks. 2. Speculation. 3. Consumer behavior. I. Keasey.
Kevin. II. Title.
HG4661.D89   1999
332.63'22--dc21   99-30109
                                                                        CIP

British Library Cataloguing in Publication Data

A catalogue record for this book is available from the British Library

ISBN 0-471-72028-3

Typeset in 10/12pt Times by Mathematical Composition Setters Ltd, Salisbury, Wiltshire.
Printed and bound in Great Britain by Bookcraft (Bath) Ltd, Midsomer Norton, Somerset.

Contents

Preface   vii

1 Preliminaries   1

2 Experimental design   9

3 The nature and success of repeated financial decisions   23

4 Do the demand curves for stocks slope downwards?   41

5 Repeated financial decisions and the leptokurtic nature of stock distributions   49

6 Conclusions   63

Appendices   69

Endnotes   77

References   79

Preface

For a variety of reasons more people have become interested in the operation of financial markets. In the UK the large number of privatisations and the de-mutualisation of building societies have made many ordinary people shareholders for the first time. The large number of financial scandals across the late 1980s to early 1990s has also focused attention on financial markets. In addition, the advent of tax breaks for a whole stream of financial instruments (for example, PEPs, Tessas, etc.) and the publication of 'money sections' by the tabloid press have led more people to consider their own personal, financial portfolios. Finally, the television and radio media report on a daily basis the performance of world economies, stock markets, exchange rates, etc. Against this background of increased public interest in the operation of financial markets, and especially equity markets, traditional main-stream finance theory has offered little in the way of insights concerning the day-to-day behaviour of stock markets. In part response to this there has been an increased emphasis within finance theory on the micro structure operations of stock markets. To date, however, this developing literature has not been able to illuminate the behaviour of stock markets or their many noted facets; for example, the tendency to volatility and extreme reaction to events.

The purpose of this monograph is to report the results of a large-scale experimental study into the types of behaviour individuals display when trading with stocks. The results indicate that individuals focus on one side of the buy/sell decision; that is, individuals show a fundamental asymmetry in the way they approach the stock market. Also, success is found to be a function of being active in the market and not being afraid to be aggressive—if the market moves, react and react with passion. Furthermore, these trading behaviours of individuals lead to elastic demand curves for stocks (an important condition for market efficiency) and they offer an explanation for the leptokurtic nature of stock returns (a noted anomaly of stock markets). In other words, the noted trading behaviours are consistent both with one aspect of market efficiency and an important empirical feature of stock markets. Given this, it is hoped that the current results are sufficiently interesting for others to want to follow the research lead offered here. If this is achieved, then we may gain greater insights into markets that are increasingly important for ever larger sections of society. Such an achievement would allow us to develop theories and understanding that move on from the simplistic notions of market efficiency and stories of 'gambling casinos'!

Finally, it goes without saying that this study owes a lot to the ideas and influence of a large set of colleagues and that all remaining errors are our own.

1 Preliminaries

1. Introduction

This study focuses on the repeated nature of one financial decision: the trading (buying and selling) of stocks on financial markets. The focus is particularly relevant because a prime characteristic of financial stock markets is the high degree of repeated decision making. Every time the price of a share changes (information signal in an efficient market) individuals are faced with a repeated decision: should they buy or sell the share? Although the financial markets are characterised by repeated decision making, there has been almost a total absence of analysis into this aspect of their operation. Essentially, mainstream finance theory makes no distinction between one-off decisions that populate so much of decision theory and the repeated decisions that characterise the financial stock markets. In making a start on this research it is intended to offer a first insight into the nature and defining characteristics of repeated decisions in the context of financial trading. Owing to the limitations of conventional empirical techniques the method of analysis adopted here is a large-scale experimental study.

Given that the purpose of this book is to describe the results of a large-scale experimental study into repeated financial trading decisions, this chapter offers a backcloth/motivation to the later chapters by comparing and contrasting the assumptions of the mainstream finance model with the characteristics of the situations likely to be faced by practical investors. It needs to be emphasised that all the issues raised in the present chapter cannot be captured within a single experimental study. Rather, it is the purpose of the present chapter to offer evidence of the need to offer a richer description of the way individuals potentially trade with stocks. The structure of the chapter is as follows. In the second section the objectives of investors are considered and this is followed in Section 3 by a review of the subjective expected utility framework that lies at the heart of finance theory. Section 4 looks at the differences between unique and repeated decisions and Section 5 considers whether stock returns are random. In Section 6 the fundamental elements of the current experimental design are discussed and the final section offers a perspective on the methodological stance of the present study.

2. The objectives of investors

One essential characteristic of the mainstream finance model is that investors are supposed to view decisions purely in terms of their impact upon the utility of their 'final' (terminal) wealth position. It is not at all clear that this is the only, or the most appropriate, description of investor objectives. Although it would be possible to draw up a fairly exhaustive set of objectives, we will confine ourselves to a single alternative example. In contrast to the mainstream finance model's assumption that investors gain utility from terminal wealth at a given point in time, some investors may gain utility from comparing their wealth to a benchmark. For individual investors the benchmark might be, for example, a wealth level beneath which they do not wish to drop. A special case is where the benchmark is their own prior level of wealth. In this regard there is an increasing literature which recognises that individuals focus on gains and losses in wealth rather than just terminal wealth (see, for example, Thaler and Johnson, 1990).

Given the focus of mainstream finance on one-off decisions made in a timeless, frictionless world, it is not surprising that a further problematic feature of the approach is that there is no explicit mechanism (apart from the assumed ability of investors to costlessly transfer wealth through time via the existence of perfect capital markets) for an investor to compare future amounts of wealth at different points in time. This is a problem for real investors because they have to make use of their wealth at different points of their lives if they are to survive and prosper. Given this, they have to be able to compare the utility of wealth at different points in time on an equal basis. If simple monetary values were being compared, such an issue would normally be solved by discounting back to a common present value. However, as mainstream finance sees investors as maximising the expected utility of their terminal wealth, it would be necessary to discount future utilities and it is not at all clear what would be the appropriate process for achieving this. The lack of an explicit time element in the mainstream model would not be a problem if individuals led static lives from birth to death; on this basis utilities from different points of time could be compared from the perspective of a fixed utility function. Individuals do not live static lives, however, and they are aware that they (and their preferences) will change as they learn, develop, prosper and fail when attempting to confront and deal with the opportunities offered by life. In this context, it is perhaps unwise to judge the stock market behaviour of individuals from the perspective of a model where the preferences of individuals are assumed to be time invariant.

In summary, utility functions that are purely a function of terminal wealth may only describe a very limited range of possible ways in which investors seek to gain utility from investment in stocks. Moreover, investors have to find ways of evaluating decisions across time—an issue the mainstream model effectively ignores.

3.   The subjective expected utility decision framework

The pre   s section questioned the description of the objectives of investors in the mainstream finance model. This section reviews the adequacy of the subjective expected utility (SEU) decision-making framework that lies at the core of modern finance theory. From the most general theoretical point of view, the SEU framework assumes that people using the approach to make decisions are able to take into account *all* possible states of the world, the probabilities of each state occurring and the consequences (in terms of utility) of each state. This level of foresight is far beyond human capabilities (see Gans, 1996). We severely doubt whether many investors would be happy with their own ability to predict patterns of returns indefinitely into the future or with the notion that simplistic mathematical models adequately represent market behaviour and/or their own utility systems. Keynes (1961) acknowledged this issue in Chapter 12 of his *General Theory*:

> We are merely reminding ourselves that human decisions affecting the future, whether personal or political or economic, cannot depend on strict mathematical expectation, since the basis for making such calculations does not exist; and that it is our innate urge to activity which makes the wheels go round, our rational selves choosing between the alternatives as best we are able, calculating where we can, but often falling back for our motive on whim or sentiment or chance (p. 162).

With regard to SEU in particular, Hey (1983) produced a cogent critique of its use as a practical guide to decision making under uncertainty. In the light of its problems, individuals may conclude that the SEU framework is not going to be a helpful method for enabling them to make decisions. Instead, they may adopt heuristics and other rules to cope with the difficulties of making decisions in the context of highly uncertain environments; for example, they may adopt what has been described by Savage (1972) as a 'Cross that Bridge When you Come to it' rule.

Essentially, given the uncertainties that come with life, it is quite a bold step to assume, as the SEU framework does, that individuals are willing and able to evaluate the utilities that are associated with the multitude of possibilities that may emerge across a lifetime. Essentially, if we are to take this assumption seriously, individuals have to be able to map out all the possible routes their lives might take up to the point of their deaths (and this ignores the intra-generational transfer issue) and be able to compute and compare (both across consequences and time) the utilities that might result from the range of consequences at any point of their lives! Von Neuman and Morgenstern (1947) themselves were not unaware of these problems as they observed that

> Evidently the common individual, whose behaviour one wants to describe, does not measure his utilities exactly but rather conducts his economic activities in a sphere of considerable haziness (p. 20).

Given the above scenario it would not be surprising if investors did not attempt fully to articulate their objectives, knowing that they may be facing changing personal (for example, gains in wealth) and market conditions (for example, an improving global economy). Even without such changes, individuals face a range of daily decisions of varying difficulty and incommensurability, and it is not a foregone conclusion that they are able to derive a fully ordered preference set/fully defined utility function (see Elster, 1979). In addition to the general points made so far, there are many particular criticisms that can be made of the SEU framework. For example, although the SEU framework uses linear functions of probabilities, there is now a substantial body of evidence (see Machina, 1987) that a range of observed behaviour cannot be modelled using linear probability functions. An example of this is the well known Allais paradox (see Allais, 1953; Allais and Hagen, 1979); that is, when faced with deciding between certain types of gambles the majority of subjects will make inconsistent choices. Similarly, within the SEU each action has its own expected utility independent of any other action. There is increasing evidence that the utilities of actions are not defined independently of each other (for example, see the work of Loomes and Sugden, 1982, 1983, on regret theory) or of the context within which the decision takes place (see Tversky and Kahneman, 1981, on framing effects). Finally, the SEU framework views a decision as a one-off event where there are no psychological costs of making the decision. It has been established by experiment (Thaler and Johnson, 1990; Wedell and Bockenholt, 1990; Joan *et al*, 1990) that individuals act differently when faced with repeated as opposed to unique decisions

4.   Unique and repeated decisions—essential differences

As noted above, the dominant framework of analysis for financial decisions is that of SEU. The calculus of expected utility is an essentially 'one shot' process where an individual requires knowledge of the (subjective) probability distribution associated with all possible outcomes and conditional outcomes. Essentially, the decision calculus of SEU is such that the expected utility of some prospect P which has a range of possible outcomes (x_1, x_i, x_n) with associated probabilities (p_1, p_i, p_n) is given by

$$EU(P) = \sum_i p_i U(x_i).$$

The value of a lottery depends, therefore, on the value of the prizes and the associated probabilities. All future possible options open to an individual are incorporated into an increasingly complex present lottery and the calculus of expected utility is, therefore, an essentially 'one shot' process. To compute the SEU of a decision, an individual requires knowledge of the (subjective) probability distribution associated with all possible outcomes and conditional outcomes. Indeed, an individual must be able to identify all conceivable and conditional outcomes. Armed with this information, the individual must solve the decision problem via backward induction. Thus, SEU is in essence a one-shot capture all (all possible future outcomes and associated probabilities are used to calculate a single expected value) decision process. Essentially, SEU advocates that unique and repeated decisions should be treated alike.

The fundamental differences between unique and repeated decisions have been discussed by McCardle and Winkler (1992). They argue, drawing on Kim (1973, p. 149), that the gains/losses associated with a decision today can affect gains/losses tomorrow because of the gambles that can be made (a wealth effect). The distinction is further exacerbated by the positive/negative signals associated with previous gains/losses (a learning effect). These compounding and learning effects raise questions over the appropriate context in which to assess utility functions. McCardle and Winkler (1992) argue that assessing utility functions by modelling small world decisions in isolation (that is, unique decisions, omitting potential future opportunities, learning, etc.) is inappropriate because, in reality, individuals face a sequence of ongoing, interrelated decisions with important implications for compounding and learning.

5. Are risky investment returns random?

A final aspect of mainstream finance that we will consider here is the assumption that returns are randomly distributed. In the broadest of terms it could be said that from approximately the early 1960s to the mid 1980s most academic opinion would have accepted that risky investment returns are largely random. On the other hand, in the same period much of the work of investment practitioners was implicitly based on the premise that returns were predictable, at least in the long term. Over approximately the last 10 years opinions have become less polarised. There is now a body of academic evidence in favour of an element of predictability in investment returns. Some practitioners, on the other hand, have accepted that predicting investment returns is a difficult task and turned to index fund management. One view that is gaining increasing acceptance is that returns display a degree of mean reversion (see Reichenstein and Dorsett, 1995, for a summary of the arguments regarding mean reversion). Clearly, whether investors believe returns to be random or, to a degree, predictable will affect the way they behave. It seems fair to conclude that there is sufficient evidence to suggest that investors would not be foolish to look for patterns in stock prices and to behave accordingly.

6. The experimental study

In pursuit of offering a richer description of the way in which individuals might trade with stocks, the current study adopts an experimental design in which individuals are faced with a series of real-world historic share prices (close of trade prices) and their task is to decide how much of their funds to invest in the share represented by the price series and how much to hold in a zero-return, no-risk alternative. Individuals face a total of five different price series from five different shares traded on the London Stock Exchange. For each price series, individuals make repeated decisions about how much to hold in the share and zero-return asset over a period of 40 minutes. After each decision the price series is moved on by one day (real world). During the 40-minute trading period, individuals could theoretically access up to five years of past share price data for each share. A detailed discussion of the experimental design, strengths and weaknesses is contained in Chapter 2. For the time being, however, it is important to point out that one of the strengths of the design is the degree of generality attainable. Thus, it is possible to investigate a greater number of interrelated issues than would be possible with a very specific and single focused design. The issues that this study purports to investigate are now introduced and a story relating these issues is given.

First, Chapter 3 considers, what decision processes do individuals adopt for their choice criteria when faced with a series of prices? Are these decision processes stationary in nature; that is, do they focus on past prices and past information? In support of the preliminary results of Ansic and Keasey (1994) this study concludes that when making repeated financial trading decisions, individuals adopt stationary decision processes even when they face non-stationary price series. A related issue is to ascertain the characteristics of successful trading strategies. The definition of the most successful trading strategy utilised here is the most profitable one. The results of this study provide evidence that the best trading strategies can be classified as possessing the '3As'; asymmetry, activity and aggression. In an attempt to ease their trading decisions, the most successful individuals adopt asymmetric strategies. This is an example of a decision heuristic intended to ease the computational problems associated with repeated financial trading. Individuals buy (or sell) a block of shares at a given reference price and then sell (or buy) at prices in excess (or below) their reference price. The use of a single reference price allows the easy determination of profitable trading opportunities that can be actively and aggressively exploited.

The study then considers whether the nature of the decision process and choice of trading strategy adopted by individuals, in aggregate, have direct implications for two fundamental issues within finance. First, their impact on the demand function faced by the traded security is considered in Chapter 4. Much of finance theory is premised on the demand curve for stocks being highly price elastic (or horizontal in the extreme). Thus, the determination of the type of demand function faced by financial stocks is of paramount importance. The previous empirical literature has been unable to address directly the price–demand relationship due to confounding influences such as event and information effects. The results indicate the demand for stocks to be price elastic and Chapter 4 considers how this might reflect the decision-making behaviour of individuals. Secondly, the implications of such trading behaviour for the price distribution properties of the securities represent the final issue of concern in this study. It is an empirical fact that recorded stock returns are leptokurtic (being overly peaked with fat tails) and Chapter 5 considers how the trading nature of individuals might explain this property. The final chapter offers a summary and conclusions.

7. Methodological stance and conclusions

This study seeks to use an experimental approach to offer a greater understanding of the way in which individuals might buy and sell stocks. Essentially, the study is attempting to offer evidence and arguments that will shift mainstream finance academics from their 'comfort zone' of internally consistent but largely irrelevant models to one where models have the potential to offer insights into the operation of financial markets and their constituent parts. The emphasis adopted here is that models must have at least a degree of descriptive validity if they are to have any hope of offering insight.

The above emphasis was drawn from the basic conclusion that many (if not all) of the assumptions of the mainstream finance model could be questioned in terms of their descriptive validity. At this juncture there is a clear need to consider whether a lack of realism in assumptions is important and to an extent this depends on the methodological perspective taken of the purpose of finance. If finance is thought of primarily as a deductive process, where conclusions are arrived at by logical deduction from a set of axioms that are claimed to be true a priori, then, in these terms, the mainstream finance model is beyond reproach. However, the tack taken here is that deduction itself is a largely arid exercise unless there is some foundation in reality, no matter how it is conceived. In other words, reality cannot be ignored when assessing the worth of a model and it is at this level that mainstream finance theory needs to take stock of the evidence.

In contrast to the above, if a strictly instrumental view of finance is taken, in line with the views of Friedman (1953), that the only test of a model is the accuracy of its predictions, then there would seem to be no real role for emphasising the importance of assumptions having descriptive validity. This perspective can, however, be questioned on at least two grounds. First, there are the implicit assumptions that there is little connection between the descriptive validity of a model's assumptions and its eventual predictive ability, and there is no cost to testing a model's predictive power. If it is accepted that there is likely to be a connection between the descriptive validity of a model's assumptions and its predictive power and that there are real costs associated with establishing a model's predictive power, then there will be merit in model building from a base that attempts to be descriptively valid. Secondly, there are models in finance (for example, the capital asset pricing model) that are not open to direct empirical testing. For models where it is not possible to confirm or falsify predictions empirically, a purely instrumental perspective would lead to the situation in which there is never a necessity to modify the given set of assumptions; indeed, mainstream finance theory could well be characterised in this vein! In such situations, relevance can only be established by considering the descriptive validity of the model's assumptions.

The above arguments could be questioned, however, if finance theory is viewed as part of a social process whereby finance theorists are seeking to persuade their chosen audience by means of rhetoric. This view does seem to reflect one aspect of mainstream finance! In this respect, the descriptive validity of a model's assumptions is only important if it affects the credibility of the rhetoric. In this particular example, it would seem that the lack of a descriptive validity of the assumptions has been important in that practitioners, in general, have not been influenced by many of the theoretical conclusions (for example, see Hudson *et al*'s discussion, 1997, of the time diversification debate).

In summary, we would argue that the descriptive validity of finance models should be recognised as being important. A greater emphasis on realism would, however, require the resolution of some problems. One obvious difficulty is that there is no unique set of assumptions that can be considered to be realistic. The most appropriate set of assumptions will depend on the particular nature of the circumstances and of the attitudes of the relevant investor group. This would undoubtedly lead to greater complexity, but this approach is surely more tenable than pretending that one set of assumptions is suitable for everyone because it is simple and elegant. Debating and explaining the need for a particular set of assumptions should facilitate a greater understanding of any given finance problem. Essentially, the time has more than passed for finance theory to place less emphasis on searching for general solutions and instead to devote more effort to developing well-grounded approaches to particular issues. In the messy and difficult world we all inhabit, which is characterised by uncertainty, transaction costs, psychological costs of decision making, habits, heuristics, etc. it is a vain hope that much insight will be gained by general and abstract models of behaviour. It is perhaps a sad fact of life for researchers of finance (given the parameters of performance measurement in their own profession) that meaningful insights will only be gained if their models are populated with assumptions that are grounded in the perceptions and actions of individuals struggling to deal with the stark realities of the financial world. It is in this vein that the following chapters offer the results of a large-scale experimental study into trading behaviour with financial stocks.

2   Experimental design

1. Introduction

This chapter is intended to give a general, but detailed, introduction to the experimental design adopted in the investigation of the four issues of concern in this study. The results and the analysis, as they relate to specific issues, are contained in separate chapters to follow. As a result, any specific points of design that relate solely to a particular issue will also be discussed in the relevant chapter to follow. A general discussion of the experimental method and associated strengths is followed by a detailed exposition of the design adopted. The chapter concludes by highlighting certain concerns and weaknesses of the experimental design. Argument is included, however, to suggest that these are not fundamental problems.

2. Experimental method

The fundamental objective of experimental economics is the creation of an environment that can be controlled, manipulated as desired and that allows accurate measurement of variables (Wilde, 1980). The limited exercise of control in field studies and the sometimes questionable validity (reliability) of field data ensure that experimentation provides superior precision. The type of experiment and the subsequent design depend upon the purpose for which the experiment is conducted. Various experimentalists offer alternative opinions as to the purposes for conducting experiments in economics (see Hey, 1992; Friedman and Sunder, 1994, Chapter 1; and Smith, 1994, for examples). However, experiments are predominantly designed to test a theoretical model via a comparison of theoretical predictions with observed outcomes. The precise control achievable over relevant variables and parameters allows the determination of the validity of a theory to be separated from the determination of whether it survives the transition from *ceteris paribus* conditions to the real world. It is also possible to design a single experiment that permits the discrimination between competing theories, again via the comparison of disparate theoretical predictions with observed experimental outcomes. However, a further distinct purpose of experimentation, and the one adopted here, is to generate, and so discover, empirical regularities that cannot be explained by existing theory, and thus provide a basis for the suggestion of new theory. Empirical observations throw up areas where the current theory is deficient, provoking theoretical development in those areas. This is fundamental to the cycle of scientific progress.

Irrespective of the purpose for which the experimental method is being used, it is essential that the experimenter is able to exercise control over important variables. Control is the substance of experimental economics and is achieved using a reward structure to induce specific monetary values on given actions and the resulting outcomes. It is, therefore, possible to control participants' preferences. However, to accomplish this an experiment must satisfy a number of sufficient conditions, which Smith (1982) terms precepts. Each of these conditions is discussed in turn.

1. *Non-satiation*: Utility is a monotone increasing function of the monetary reward, thus an autonomous individual will choose (prefer) the action with the highest reward. Such individuals do not become satiated and always act so as to increase their level of the monetary reward.
2. *Saliency*: To have a motivational effect the reward structure must be related to the actions of individuals; thus, an individual's reward will depend upon the action chosen. A fixed payment for participation is not salient, because it is not dependent upon the actions and resultant observed outcomes of individuals. However, a monetary reward related to (say) the level of experimental profit earned is salient and motivates individuals to choose actions that maximise the level of experimental profit earned.
3. *Dominance*: To guarantee control over an individual's preferences, the reward structure must suppress any subjective costs associated with that individual's participation in the experiment. Consequently, the overwhelming influence on an individual's utility from participating derives from the monetary reward structure. This is most likely to be the case the higher is the salient monetary reward. Thus, the increase in monetary reward that an individual experiences as a result of a given action dominates any other influence on that individual's choice of action.
4. *Privacy*: Subjects are given information only with respect to their own payoff alternatives, thus there is incomplete information. The potential for loss of induced value (preference) due to interdependent utilities is eradicated. Thus, irrespective of whether participants care about the reward earned by others, the removal of such information via privacy ensures that the induced value is solely the result of the individual's own monetary rewards.
5. *Parallelism*: Parallelism occurs when the conclusions drawn from the experiment are equally valid for field data under similar *ceteris paribus* conditions.

The first four of the above precepts provide for controlled microeconomic experiments and ensure the achievement of control over participants' characteristics. It is viable to impose any relationship between a participant's decision and the monetary reward, thus inducing value upon the decision choice. This induced value will hold providing that the relationship is made explicit to the subjects (saliency), who are motivated by the monetary reward (non-satiation and monotonicity) rather than other confounding influences (dominance and privacy). These conditions are sufficient to ensure that control is exercised in the experiment. The parallelism precept allows the conclusion to be drawn that the experimental results carry over into the field.

3. The experimental design

The first dilemma to rear its head when determining the specific design of an experiment is whether to pursue a policy of realism, and so mimic reality as accurately as is possible, or to reproduce precisely the specifications detailed in the theory under investigation. Friedman and Sunder (1994, p. 10) argue that neither of these polar extremes is singularly appropriate. It is impossible to capture all the intricacies of the natural environment in an experimental design. Even if the theory is so explicit as to allow exact replication in the laboratory, this too is unproductive. There is no scope for learning, because observations consistent with the predictions of the theory only provide evidence that there is no logical flaw in the theory and only offer limited evidence of the theory's predictive ability. Thus, Friedman and Sunder (1994, p. 12) conclude that '...a laboratory experiment should be judged by its impact on our understanding, not by its fidelity either to reality or to a formal model'. In light of these comments, the lack of any definitive model of repeated financial decision making and the previously stated purpose of this study to explore the nature of repeated financial decisions, the current design strikes a middle ground. The specifics of the design are now introduced.

To recap, the four related issues of concern that this study addresses are

1. the decision processes underlying individuals' repeated financial decisions,
2. the characteristics of successful trading strategies,
3. the derivation of the demand function faced by financial stocks and
4. the distributional properties of the price series.

Given the wide area covered by these related issues, it must be recognised that the choice of experimental design must be made carefully so that the design itself is not so specific that it restricts the scope of analysis. It is clear, therefore, that some form of trade-off will be apparent. A general design that allows several important issues of concern to be investigated will offer a little less control than could be achieved using separate, specific designs for each separate issue in turn. The literature on repeated financial decisions is very much in its infancy and so this study is intended to be exploratory in nature and design. A conscious decision was, therefore, made to accept some loss of experimental control in order to allow an investigation of much wider issues of importance. It is intended that these exploratory results guide future research.

In the experimental literature investigating financial asset markets, the general approach has been to conduct micro-auctions in which participants trade, and endogenously determine the price of, financial assets (see Plott and Sunder, 1982, 1988, for specific examples or Sunder, 1995, for a review of the literature). Given the predominance of the double auction as the trading institution on the world's financial and commodity markets, many studies have conducted micro-double auctions. The double auction permits traders to be both buyers *and* sellers simultaneously, submitting bids and asks for standardised units of a well defined asset (security or commodity). For discussions on the double auction institution, theoretical and experimental analysis, see Friedman and Rust (1993). The major strength of this type of experimental design is the strict control it permits over relevant parameters. Thus, the experimenter is able to test a particular theoretical model without violating any of the *ceteris paribus* conditions stipulated in the model's development. The current experimental design departs from the generally adopted design because of the exploratory nature of the study. The lack of theoretical discussion in the area of repeated financial decisions means that the strict experimental control achievable in the above design is no longer necessary or a major strength. In fact, the above design is inappropriate, given the intention of the study, because it focuses on aggregate market behaviour and generates an insufficient number of trades per session. The large volume of data required to conduct an exploratory behavioural investigation such as this would require numerous experimental sessions (including repeats of cell designs) to be conducted at prohibitively high costs. As a consequence, this study adopts a different experimental design. The underlying strategy of the current experiment is to record the buying/selling quantity responses of participants to the changing (exogenous) prices of a real-world, financial stock. The strength of this design is the large volume of data generated at a relatively low cost, both in terms of time and finance. However, the reverse of this coin is some loss of experimental control. Each time a participant is faced with a change in price he/she must decide whether to buy, sell or do nothing. Each decision will, therefore, impact on future decisions via an influence on a participant's wealth in terms of his/her holding of 'risky' shares and 'safe' money, which is no longer strictly controlled. A conscious trade-off was made to sacrifice strict experimental control for the sake of greater data generation and an exploratory analysis of the dynamic nature of repeated financial decisions.

A similar study in terms of design and, to a limited degree, focus is Andreassen (1988) in which support was found for the hypothesis that large price changes cause heavy trading volume. The design allowed participants to trade shares freely based on predetermined price data. Whilst participants were informed that all the stocks used were real, the price series were manipulated to generate 18 series that differed with respect to high/low variance and bear/bull/stable characteristics based on three different original price patterns (that is, based on the historical price series of three different shares). In addition, all the price series were standardised to begin at 35 cents. Participants were initially endowed with $4.90, comprised of 50% shares and 50% stocks (equivalent to seven stocks). Each participant faced 120 trials in the form of two blocks of 60 high-variance and 60 low-variance trials, the order of which was reversed for half the participants. The design was conducted manually with the experimenter showing participants both the price level and change on a card. Each trial lasted for approximately 30 seconds, with 20 seconds for the participant to come to a decision regarding whether or not to trade and 10 seconds for the experimenter to code and enact the decision. Participants traded more times and more shares in the high-variance price series. Most individuals followed 'tracking strategies' (buying when the price falls and selling when it rises). However, only tracking in the high-variance interval yielded high levels of profit. In a second experiment, Andreassen (1988) manipulated the stimulus individuals received, providing participants with either price levels *or* price changes, rather than both as in the previous experiment. Those participants receiving the price levels stimulus were able to track well in the high-variance interval but poorly in the low-variance interval. However, those participants receiving the price change stimulus were poor trackers in all cases. In a related study, Andreassen and Kraus (1990) examine individuals' judgemental forecasting of time-series data. Evidence is provided in support of the adoption of judgemental extrapolation models, whereby individuals' forecasts are based primarily on past observation of the variable they intend to forecast (for example, the price of a share). The essentials of the design in the second study are effectively the same as in the first. The intention of the present study is to extend the previous research in a number of ways. First, the manipulation of the price series data in Andreassen (1988) and Andreassen and Kraus (1990) was for the specific purpose of investigating the impact of price variance on trading volume, amongst other things. This study is concerned with a more general analysis of trading behaviour and so uses raw price series data without any manipulation. None of the price series has been constructed so as to represent high or low variance, or bear, bull or stable markets. Thus, there are no artificial trends in the data that participants could exploit to determine trading strategies. Secondly, the use of exactly 120 trials in the previous studies was deemed to be a limiting factor in the analysis of repeated financial decisions. Consequently, there was no set number of prices that participants could access. The total number of prices viewed, and so decisions made, was entirely dependent on the speed at which each individual came to a decision. Therefore, the third area of divergence from the previous studies is the removal of the 30-second set trial duration that effectively imposed artificial time pressure on the decision problem.

There now follows a detailed discussion of the general experimental design adopted, under the subheadings of task, price series, participants, motivation/payoff design and issues of design.

Task

After an initial practice round, the main body of the experiment consisted of 62 participants individually buying and selling a stock during a trading period of 40 minutes on each of five consecutive days (real time). During each trading period the participants sat at a trading screen for 40 minutes and with the aid of written instructions (see Appendix I) had to buy/sell the identified blue-chip stock. The trading screen (Figure 2.1a) facing each participant consisted of a past history of the daily closing prices of the stock, an opening inventory of stocks (75 in number), the current stock price and a trading box in which he/she could buy/sell or view the past prices of the stock. Figure 2.1(b) displays the type of view screen the participants could access throughout their trading periods. The computer program recomputed the wealth position after each trade. A participant's task, therefore, consists of adjusting his/her holdings of both shares and cash in the light of fluctuating prices of the 'risky' share. The 'riskless' asset cash offers a zero rate of return. Participants did not incur financial transaction costs whenever they traded. However, if they chose to leave their portfolio unadjusted and see the next price in the series they incurred a 3-second time cost. That is, there was a 3-second delay before they could enact their next decision.

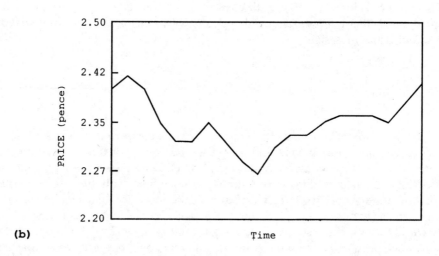

```
 0.00
 2.40   2.33
 2.42   2.35
 2.40   2.36
 2.35   2.36
 2.32   2.36
 2.32   2.35
 2.35   2.38
 2.32   2.41
 2.29
 2.27
 2.31
 2.33
```

Figure 2.1   (a) Price history for Argyle PLC; (b) Share prices, Argyle PLC, last 20 periods

Price series

The price series faced by the participants consisted of real quoted closing price data for a given share each day. A different blue-chip UK share was chosen for each of the five trading days. (The stocks provided for each day of the experiment were British

Petroleum (practise session), Argyle PLC (day 1), Coats Viyella PLC (day 2), Allied Lyons PLC (day 3), Cadbury PLC (day 4) and Boots PLC (day 5). The closing prices used in the experiment (excluding the practise session) are graphed over time in Figure 2.2.) This was to ensure that the participants realised that they were trading with real share price data. They did not know, however, which period the prices were drawn from or which shares they would face before they sat down at the computer terminal each day. In other words, it is inconceivable that the participants would have had prior knowledge of the price series they faced on each of the trading days. In terms of each trading period, each time a participant made a decision to buy, sell or do nothing (to buy/sell nothing), he/she moved the price series on to the next price with the last price becoming part of the available price history. The top part of the trading screen could include up to 99 of the most recent prices. Figure 2.3(a) illustrates that when buying more of the share, the participant had to enter how much cash he/she wanted to spend. The computer would then calculate how many units of the share he/she had bought at the current share price and return any remaining cash to his/her cash holdings. In terms of selling units of the share, Figure 2.3(b) indicates that participants had to enter the number of units they wanted to sell at the current price. The computer would then adjust the holdings of the share down and the holdings of cash up accordingly. Alternatively, a participant could actively decide that he/she did not wish to trade (adopt a 'wait-and-see' policy) at the current price by entering the decision to either buy or sell zero. In this situation, the computer would impose a 3-second time delay and then move the price series on to the next price (see Figure 2.3c). The valuation of the portfolio would be updated without altering the balance between cash and share. Thus, the participants were able to move through the price series by deciding to buy/sell or do nothing with an associated 3-second transaction cost (our imposed price of information) for an active wait-and-see decision. The subjects were, therefore, able to move at their own optimum rate through the program while retaining the opportunity to pursue a 'wait-and-see' policy if they so wished. In addition, subjects could be completely inactive if

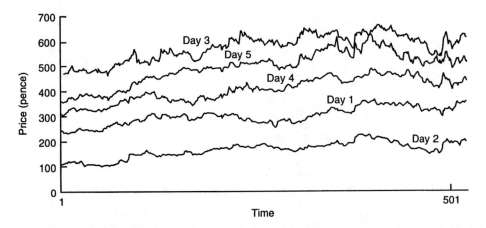

Figure 2.2   Stock price series data

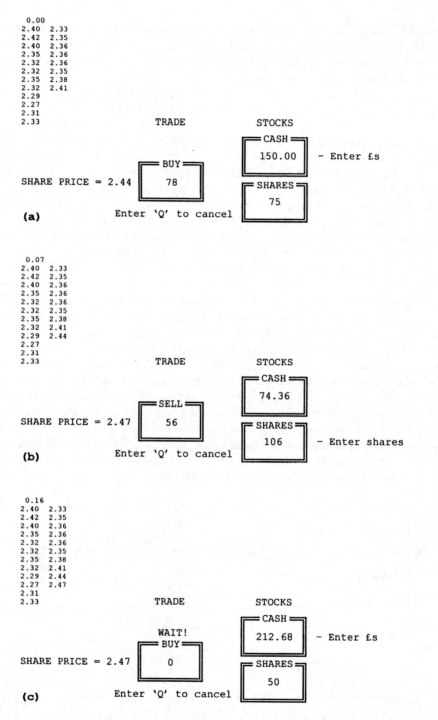

Figure 2.3 Price history for Argyle PLC; (a) buying; (b) selling; (c) 'wait and see'

they wished (an out-of-the-market strategy) but this brought with it the risk of not benefiting from improved prices on the current holding of the share. Nevertheless, this is a legitimate strategy for an individual who is satisfied with his/her current level of wealth and the design of the experiment allowed for this feature of markets.

Participants

Sixty-two undergraduate and postgraduate students took part in the experiment across five consecutive days from 26 to 30 August, 1993. The participants were drawn from the entire population of the University of Leeds, with the majority of the University's 52 departments represented by at least one participant. Owing to the physical limitation on the number of participants in the computer cluster at any one time (a maximum number of 24) and the insurmountable logistical problems regarding individuals' timetables, participants could drop in to the computer cluster to complete their sessions at any convenient time between 9.00 a.m. and 5.00 p.m., during each of the five days of the experiment.

Motivation/payoff design

One of the most difficult aspects of experimental design is to make participation attractive while ensuring that the task is taken seriously across its various dimensions. In the present context, the participants were told they would receive £0.03 for each £1 increase in their wealth position. At the end of each trading period they liquidated their trading position and this final wealth position was used to compute their prize money for the day. Although each trading day began with an initial wealth of £150 and 75 shares, prize money gains for one day could be offset by prize money losses from another trading day. In other words, it was possible for a participant to walk away from five days of trading with nothing to show for his/her effort. In fact, the minimum prize for the overall experiment was £0.45. Nonetheless, from the base of risk-neutral simulations and the experience of a pilot study, the payoff scheme was designed to pay out approximately £4.00 per participant per trading period (£6.00 per hour equivalent) on each day. This level of payment was designed to be attractive to students on a weekly grant of approximately £38. To ensure completion of the entire experiment (all five days) participants were not paid until completion of the fifth day's session. Equally, to ensure participation in such a lengthy experiment, there was no possibility within the current design for participants to lose some of their own wealth. From a purist perspective this is a weakness of the payoff design but one that is common to a large number of experiments. Finally, to increase the probability of achieving a good response to the request for participants, there was a final prize of £100 to the person who achieved the biggest increase in wealth across the five days of trading. Therefore, the sums available as payoffs in the current experiment are not insubstantial when compared with the weekly incomes of students.

In summary, the experiment was designed to capture the nature of the repeated financial decision making of active investors within a trading environment. Participants were motivated fully to disclose their responses to the changing prices of a share. An analysis of these responses allows direct conclusions to be drawn concerning the nature of the trading behaviour of individuals. These quantity responses also allow a direct examination of the nature of the demand curve for shares of noisy traders. The experimental design further permits consideration of the price distribution properties of securities. By providing price series that differed in terms of their levels, ranges and degrees of volatility, the experiment was designed to ensure robust results. An additional benefit of the experiment containing five days of trading was that it allowed the participants to become fully conversant with the general decision making environment.

4. Experimental design concerns: A justification

This section opens with a brief consideration of generally voiced criticisms of experimental methods as they relate to the current study, after which the discussion turns to an evaluation of specific design concerns in an attempt to provide a justification for the choice of design.

A fundamental criticism of experiments in economics focuses on their simplicity. Experiments are too simple to describe the real world, which is a far more complex phenomenon. However, as argued by Hey (1992, p. 91), if the intention of the experiment is to replicate the domain of a theory and test its predictions, then *a fortiori* the theory is too simple. The lack of realism reflects parameters that are absent from the theory. Thus, if this criticism is taken at all seriously it also casts a shadow over the associated theoretical analysis. In fact, simplicity may be a virtue of experimentation rather than a weakness, because it permits a clear interpretation of the observed behaviour. If the theory fails to predict observed behaviour in a simple setting, then its validity in a more complex environment is fundamentally questioned. Owing to their simplicity, experiments are artificial and abstract from reality. It is possible, therefore, to suggest that individuals will behave differently in the real world. Hey (1991, p. 13) 'counters this by arguing that, in experiments, the subjects (who are undoubtedly real) are tackling a real problem for real money, that their payment depends on their decisions and that everything about it is real'. Thus, the claim that experiments are not real is countered by having participants tackle a real (but stripped down) decision situation for real money.

Another general criticism of experiments is that participants are thrown into strange environments and are not given a chance to learn. To counter such a possibility, the current experiment made the written, verbal and computer based instructions clear and easily accessible. In addition, the participants had the ability to ask points of clarification during an extensive practise session. Furthermore, the experiment was run over five consecutive days to avoid any problems of non-familiarity with the decision environment. The discussion will now consider specific concerns of the current experimental design.

At its most general, the trading behaviour of individuals should be derived in an environment where there are many commodities/shares. Thus, a criticism of the design might be an absence of a general portfolio of stocks from which to trade. This is, of course, difficult to operationalise experimentally. Previous studies by Kroll *et al* (1988a, b) incorporated experimental designs in which participants were able to trade in two or three shares, with or without the existence of a riskless asset. However, these studies were intended to investigate the predictions of the capital asset pricing model and the mean-variance model in the context of portfolio selection, and as such were not designed specifically with the nature of repeated financial decisions in mind. In both designs participants took part in 10 games consisting of 5 or 10 trials. In each trial their decision task was to allocate capital between a small number of risky shares and a riskless asset (not included in all sessions). It is clear, therefore, that the designs used in Kroll *et al* (1988a, b) do not permit a detailed analysis of the nature of repeated financial decisions. Owing to the increased degree of complexity arising from the extended decision horizon in the current study and as a result of the obvious need to maintain a certain degree of simplicity, the experimental design adopted here only allows participants to substitute the riskless asset cash for the one traded share. Thus, there is no portfolio of risky assets that individuals are able to hold. The exact impact of this feature of the experiment on trading behaviour is difficult to determine a priori. One possible consequence is that trading may be biased downwards because of the lack of close substitutes. In contrast, with only a single share being available, trading may be increased because attention is focused solely on the given share.

The experiment might be argued to be unrealistic because the size and direction of trades have no impact on the next market price faced. This reflects, however, the atomistic price-taking framework at the heart of competitive financial markets. Indeed, if individual participants could commonly affect prices via their trades, then the essential stability of markets would be called into question because of the presence of 'money pumps'. Hence, the price series is exogenous and there is no link between the actions of agents and the price series. Similarly, the experiment might be accused of creating an environment where traders never trade with others (or anybody). As before, however, this reflects the atomistic nature of financial markets: neither personalities nor reputations enter the trading process; individual agents simply buy/sell at the given market price.

A third possible issue of concern is that the riskless asset cash offers a zero rate of return and this may be seen, at first sight, to bias the results. However, given the research is concerned with the nature of trading behaviour rather than with the absolute level of trading, it is not clear how a zero return to the riskless asset would bias the results. A conscious attempt was made to allow the participants to focus on the implicit risk and return characteristics of the tradable stock. From the price information available, individuals were confronted with a series of difficult decisions under uncertainty. It was felt that little would be gained by adding the complication of a return to the riskless asset. Furthermore, it is difficult to see how the results would be affected by a zero rate of return as compared with the present real rate of return of 2% to 3%. It is for these reasons and because of its simplicity that a zero rate of return was chosen for the riskless asset. Potential effects of this simplification could be fruitfully investigated in future work.

A fourth potential criticism is that the absence of transaction costs (with the exception of the notional transaction cost of a 3-second time delay when an individual chooses to move the price series on without a decision to buy or sell having been made) within the experiment will have biased trading behaviour. There is no doubt that an absence of transaction costs can only have increased the propensity to trade. However, it must be remembered that absolute levels of trade were not a focus of concern in the current study. Furthermore, given the presence of differing transaction costs in stock markets across the globe and an absence of knowledge over the exact impact of transaction costs on trading behaviour, it was decided to have no real transaction costs in the present analysis as this establishes one fixed point in the range of possibilities. Future experimental work could usefully establish the impact of transaction costs on trading behaviour.

As with most experimental designs, there are always trade-offs to be made. For example, in ensuring familiarity with the experiment, we had to balance sample size with possible 'contamination effects'. To maintain a reasonable sample size we decided to give the participants the freedom to choose what time they attended the experiment on a given day. In addition, the computer cluster available to us across the five days had a maximum of 24 places at any one time. This means of ensuring a sufficient sample size (confounded by timetable logistics of the participants) and meeting the size constraint of the available computer cluster ran the risk of early participants informing later participants of the nature of the price series to be faced that day. None the less, whilst this potential cannot be denied, we conclude the risk of collusion to be minimal, based on a number of reasons. First, the complexity and volume of the price series data that confronted participants each day was such that it is inconceivable that any one individual could provide another with detailed information concerning the price series. Depending on their rate of decision making, participants could witness in the region of 500+ prices in a given 40-minute trading period day. There is little possibility of their remembering more than the last dozen or so prices. Even if they did pass this information on to a co-colluder, to profit from such information would require the second individual to attain exactly the same point in the price series, during the 40 minutes, as the first individual. This would be highly unlikely, given the disparate decision-making time required by different individuals. Casual observation of the data shows that participants finished the 40-minute trading periods at widely dispersed points in the price series on any given day. It is still conceivable that individuals were able to convey the general trend in the price series of a given day, information that could be profitably exploited by other co-colluders. However, potential for this type of behaviour is dramatically reduced by the fact that participants were drawn from the majority of the 52 departments that comprise the large campus of the University of Leeds. Lastly, participants were involved in a competitive situation with a sizeable monetary prize. It is disputable that knowledge of the general price series trend would be sufficient to guarantee colluders the winning prize.

It could also be argued that a final prize of £100 would have the consequence of inducing extreme trading behaviour due to tournament effects, generating a bias in the results. Whether the inclusion of a prize would result in more aggressive or more cautious trading behaviour than would otherwise have been observed is unclear.

Certain participants may have become more risk-seeking in an attempt to win the prize. However, others may have adopted a more cautious approach so that their profit level increased steadily over the five days, thus negating the possibility that one erroneous trade would wipe out all the good work done in previous days. Whilst this type of effect would undoubtedly bias the results, such behaviour should have been reduced by the fact that the participants were not fully aware of their relative trading performance. As the experiment was run via open sessions across the whole of five days, it was difficult for the participants to assess relative performance at any one point in time. Furthermore, the selection of the participants from a broad range of departments across campus should have hampered comparison via personal discussion. Thus, it would have been difficult for individuals to judge the relative benefits of following a particular trading strategy. As previously argued, any experimental design is a compromise. The £100 prize was introduced to attract a large number of participants to take part in a lengthy, time-consuming experiment. It has to be recognised, however, that the introduction of such an incentive may have had unforeseen consequences for the eventual results and further research could usefully drop the incentive to establish its impact.

To summarise, the above discussion has highlighted a number of potential concerns regarding the chosen experimental design that may lead some to question the degree of control exercised during the experiment. However, included in the discussion is an acknowledgement of a conscious choice to accept some loss of control in order to conduct a widespread exploratory analysis of repeated financial decisions and related issues. Specific potential areas of concern were discussed and justification provided to support the belief that these were not fundamental issues of concern. To conclude, Smith's (1982) four precepts of controlled experiments were adhered to in the experimental design. Participants were compensated with *salient* monetary rewards (*non-satiation*) of a level greater than their marginal wage rate (*dominance*). Owing to the disparate academic backgrounds of the participants, ranging from the majority of the 52 departments that comprise the University of Leeds, the possibility for discussion of relative performance was severely hampered, thus individuals only had information concerning their own performance (*privacy*). Smith's (1982) fifth precept, *parallelism*, is equally valid. Whilst the experimental task may have been a simplified version of that faced by individuals in the real world, it has previously been argued that experiments cannot, and should not, mirror exactly the complexity of the real-world decision environment. Simplicity is a strength of the experimental method that does not prevent the transferability of the results from the laboratory to the real world.

3 The nature and success of repeated financial decisions

1. Introduction

The focus of this chapter is the fundamental issue of interest in the present study; namely, how do individuals make repeated decisions in a financial context? An equally interesting research question is also addressed. What are the characteristics of successful decision processes in the context of repeated financial decisions? The structure of the chapter is as follows. The following section highlights the importance of the distinction between unique and repeated decisions in general, drawing on the discussion in Chapter 1. Section 3 introduces relevant literature fundamental in motivating and shaping the direction of the present study. The arguments in this section are used to guide the development of very tentative conjectures. Section 4 builds on Chapter 2, introducing specifics of the experimental design as they relate to an investigation into the nature and success of repeated financial decision making. Section 5 presents the results of this exploratory analysis. The section is split between the nature of repeated decision making and the characteristics of successful repeated decision processes. The final section contains discussion and conclusions.

2. Unique vs. repeated decisions

Some of the discussion in Chapter 1 was centred around the distinction between unique and repeated decisions. Argument was presented, concluding that the two should not be treated alike. Given that SEU does not distinguish between unique and repeated decisions, it was argued that the model was an inadequate description of the nature of the repeated decision process. Given the discussion in Chapter 1, there now follows a brief review of some of the relevant literature.

The fundamental differences between unique and repeated decisions have been discussed by McCardle and Winkler (1992). They argue, drawing on Kim (1973, p. 149), that the gains/losses associated with a decision today can affect gains/losses tomorrow because of the gambles that can be made (a wealth effect). The distinction is further exacerbated by the positive/negative signals associated with previous gains/losses (a learning effect). These compounding and learning effects raise questions over the appropriate context in which to assess utility functions. In a world of repeated dichotomous outcomes (for example, the toss of a coin) McCardle and Winkler (1992, p. 813) suggest that a learning effect distinguishes two segments of the derived utility function. The result is a discontinuous utility function. Many gambles (and specifically investments), however, involve a continuum of outcomes (for example, any percentage increase or decrease in return). In such a scenario, McCardle and Winkler (1992, p. 815) argue that whilst the derived utility function is no longer discontinuous, there will be a very steep segment that gives the impression of a smoothed version of discontinuity. Thus, the general behaviour will be qualitatively similar in many respects. There are important implications for the appropriate context in which to assess utility functions. McCardle and Winkler (1992) argue that assessing utility functions by modelling small-world decisions in isolation (that is, unique decisions, omitting potential future opportunities, learning etc.) is inappropriate because, in reality, individuals face a sequence of ongoing, interrelated decisions with important implications for compounding and learning. It would be preferable then to assess utility functions via a complex model of the grand world faced by the decision maker. Whilst possible in theory, such a complex model would be prohibitively difficult to achieve in practice.

The applicability of the SEU model in the above scenario is highly questionable. Thaler and Johnson (1990) point out that in the representation of the decision problem, SEU assumes that all possible future outcomes are integrated with current wealth and so the decision becomes one of evaluating gambles in terms of their final end states. It is only possible, therefore, for prior outcomes to influence choice via a wealth effect. Thus, the influence of learning from positive/negative signals (prior outcomes), as advocated by McCardle and Winkler (1992), is not captured by the SEU model. The importance of learning cannot be ignored.[1] Studies by Thaler and Johnson (1990) and Keasey and Moon (1996) show that prior gains/losses can dramatically influence subsequent choices in systematic ways. Under some circumstances, a prior gain can increase a subject's willingness to accept gambles (the house money effect). In contrast, prior losses can decrease the willingness to take risks.

There is growing empirical evidence that indicates that unique and repeated events should not be treated alike. For example, Wedell and Bockenholt (1990) indicate that preference reversals are reduced with multiple gambles and Joan *et al* (1990) indicate that risk may be perceived (and estimated) differently under unique and repeated conditions. The latter study was set in the context of an industrial purchasing task and so provides evidence for the generality of the unique vs. repeated distinction. In fact, the stated purpose in Keren (1991) is to substantiate further the meaningful distinction between unique and repeated gambles.[2]

To summarise, there exists a very real distinction between an individual's behaviour under unique and repeated decisions. A prime characteristic of the distinction between the two is the learning effect associated with prior outcomes as signals of future outcomes in the repeated decision scenario. The assumptions and calculus of the SEU model are such that it is unable to incorporate this important characteristic. It is therefore an inapplicable model for describing the nature of repeated decision making. In a condemning study of betweenness property[3] tests with very simple financial decisions (unique lotteries), Evans *et al* (1991) conclude that even in their extremely simplified decision scenarios, violations of SEU are such that finance theory must determine whether a more general descriptive model of financial decision making is applicable. Given the questionable validity of SEU as a descriptive model of financial decision making in simplified settings and inapplicability of the model in repeated decision scenarios, the present study is intended as an exploration of the nature and success of decision processes in repeated financial decisions. The decision scenario utilised is something akin to a repeated version of the continuous outcome gamble/investment in McCardle and Winkler (1992). The following section introduces relevant literature in order to position and motivate the present research agenda.

3. Prior literature

Kroll *et al* (1988a) devised a computer-controlled, multi-stage portfolio selection task designed to test experimentally the assumptions of the separation theorem and the capital asset pricing model (CAPM).[4] Two experiments were conducted in which participants were required to allocate actual amounts of money in a series of portfolio tasks. In task A, participants faced 10 identical and mutually independent portfolio selection problems with a maximum of 10 trials in each. In each trial, participants had to choose to invest in one or more of three risky assets with normal distributions that differed with respect to the mean and standard deviation of returns. Participants were fully informed about the parameters of the three return distributions and associated correlations. The return on the assets for each trial was determined by an independent draw from the return distributions. An initial endowment of wealth at the beginning of trial 1 was not reinitialised until the end of trial 10, thus for each trial (after the first) in a given portfolio selection problem an individual's wealth was determined endogenously. Task B was identical to task A except that participants were additionally able to invest in, or borrow from, a riskless asset at a rate of 2%. To summarise, Kroll *et al*'s (1988a, p. 515) findings cast serious doubt on the validity of both the separation theorem and the capital asset pricing model. They conjecture that individuals might have searched for patterns in the returns over time. This is supported by participants' repeated requests for information about past returns despite having perfect knowledge of the parameters governing the returns of the assets. Kroll *et al* (1988a, p. 512) suggest that '[s]ystematic studies of this possibility are warranted'.

In a related study, Kroll *et al* (1988b) adopt a similar experimental design to that above, but with only two risky assets (the returns differed with respect to mean and standard deviation and were independently and identically distributed) and one riskless asset (3% return) for all trials. The intention was to test specifically predictions derived from the mean-variance (MV) model. Participants were forced to choose between a portfolio mix of either one risky asset and the riskless asset or the other risky asset and the riskless asset, but no combination of both risky assets at once. The results were not very supportive of the MV model, with 26% of portfolio selections defined as inefficient. In line with the above related paper, Kroll *et al* (1988b, p. 407) report a 'high rate of requests for useless, but costless information'. Once more, Kroll *et al* (1988b) suggest that this may be indicative of individuals searching for patterns in the returns over time. In an attempt to address this issue they investigate sequential effects by observing the number of switches from one risky asset to the other. In total, the risky asset was switched on approximately 30%

of trials. Out of the 15 participants, 10 exhibited a negative recency effect (the 'gambler's fallacy' of holding the asset that performed relatively poorly in the belief that it will improve on the next trial), whilst the remaining five exhibited a positive recency effect, holding the asset that performed best on the preceding trial.

The above two studies generate an interesting question: What decision processes are individuals adopting to determine their portfolio selection when they frequently request information about past returns and switch from one risky asset to another on the basis of previous returns? One possible explanation would be that individuals adopt stationary decision processes when faced with repeated financial decisions. Unfortunately, the experimental design utilised in Kroll *et al* (1998a, b) is not ideal for an investigation of this possibility. In the former study, participants face a maximum of only 10 trials in each portfolio selection problem before the parameters change. In the latter study, the number of trials drops to a maximum of five trials. The number of repetitions (trials) is, therefore, too small to allow an analysis of repeated decision processes. It was emphasised to participants that their purpose was to maximise profit in each game separately. This would have expressly focused participants' attention on the 10 or five trials at a time, further reducing the notion of repeated decision making. It is the intention of the present study to address specifically the stationarity of decision processes adopted under repeated financial decision scenarios and the characteristics of successful strategies. To further this position and to provide support for the choice of experimental design, two additional papers are now introduced.

Andreassen (1988) provides strong experimental support for the hypothesis that large price changes cause heavy trading volume on stock markets. To arrive at this conclusion the study employs a design that requires participants to trade shares freely on the basis of real price data that have been manipulated to generate high/low variance and different trend-characteristic price series. From the historical price series of three different shares, 18 series were generated that differed with respect to high/low variance and bear/bull/stable characteristics. The price series were standardised to begin at 35 cents. Participants were initially endowed with $4.90, comprised of 50% shares and 50% stocks (equivalent to seven stocks). Each participant faced 120 trials in the form of two blocks of 60 high-variance and 60 low variance trials. Half the participants faced low- followed by high-variance price series, whilst for the other half the order was reversed. In the first experiment conducted, designed to investigate the high/low variance treatment, the experimenter manually showed participants both the price level and change on a card. Each trial lasted for approximately 30 seconds, with 20 seconds for the participant to come to a decision regarding whether or not to trade and 10 seconds for the experimenter to code and enact the decision. Participants traded more times and more shares in the high-variance price series compared with the low-variance series. Andreassen (1988) also reports that most individuals followed 'tracking strategies' (buying when the price falls and selling when it rises). However, only tracking in the high-variance interval yielded high levels of profit. The tracking of price was interpreted as an indication that participants paid greater attention to the price level than the price change. In a second, computerised experiment, Andreassen (1988) manipulated the stimulus individuals received, providing participants with either price levels *or* price changes, rather than both as in the previous experiment. These were the only two changes between the two experiments. Those participants receiving the price levels stimulus were able to track well in the high-variance interval but poorly in the low-variance interval. However, those participants receiving the price change stimulus were poor trackers in all cases. Andreassen (1988, p. 386) concludes that the type of strategy employed and the level of profits attained depend on the manner in which the price stimulus is presented.

In a related study, Andreassen and Kraus (1990) examine individuals' judgemental forecasting of time-series data. Evidence is provided in support of the adoption of judgemental extrapolation models, whereby individuals' forecasts are based primarily on past observation of the variable they intend to forecast (for example, the price of a share). The essentials of the design for the three experiments of the study are effectively the same as in Andreassen (1988). The exception is the first experiment, which requires participants to explicitly forecast a price series, whereas experiments 2 and 3 conduct stock market simulations, the experimental design of which is similar to that utilised in Andreassen (1988). The finding that extrapolation models are better approximations of individuals' judgemental forecasting processes provides further motivation for the intention of the current study to address specifically the stationarity of decision processes adopted under repeated financial decision scenarios and the characteristics of successful strategies.

Andreassen (1988, p. 386) states '[m]uch research is needed to establish the severity of the flaws in the judgement and choice processes of real investors.' The current study moves one step along the path to understanding the second of these issues via the determination of individuals' decision (choice) processes in the context of repeated financial decisions. Previous research is extended in a number of ways. First, the manipulation of the price series data in Andreassen (1988) and Andreassen and Kraus (1990) was for the specific purpose of investigating the impact of price variance on trading volume, amongst other things. The present study is concerned with a more general analysis of individuals' trading behaviour and decision processes and so uses raw price series data without any manipulation. The investor in the real world is seldom faced with a price series that exhibits a significantly prolonged and pronounced stable degree of either high or low variance, thus none of the price series has been constructed so as to represent high or low variance, or bear, bull or stable markets. Thus, there are no artificial trends in the data that participants could exploit to determine trading strategies. The experimental design permits a more robust investigation of individuals' decision processes. Secondly, the use of exactly 120 trials in the previous studies was deemed to be a limiting factor in the analysis of repeated financial decisions. Consequently, the current study does not exogenously set the number of prices accessible to participants. The total number of prices viewed, and so decisions made, was entirely dependent upon the speed at which each individual came to a decision. Therefore, the third area of divergence from the previous studies is the removal of the 30-second set trial duration that effectively imposed artificial time pressure on the decision problem. This artificial time constraint may have compelled participants to adopt simple decision processes such as extrapolation models. In investigating the adoption of stationary decision processes, the current study rightly omits this source of potential bias. A final potential bias was introduced in the above two studies when participants were informed that in order to increase their wealth they must buy shares for less than they sell them and to sell them before they go down. Whilst the exact impact this statement had on a participant's decision process is unclear, it is conceivable that the statement may have induced a 'disposition effect' (Shefrin and Statman, 1985, p. 777) with the tendency 'to sell winners too early and hold losers too long'. The current study avoids this potential bias by stating that a participant's task is to increase his/her wealth by trading.

The research question addressed here is: How do individuals react when faced with repeated decision scenarios and what decision processes do they adopt? Consideration is also given to the characteristics of successful decision strategies. One answer may be that individuals develop heuristics to provide decision aids that are backward looking in nature, as opposed to the forward-looking SEU model. In the context of repeated financial trading decisions, such heuristics would focus on the history of past prices. As a result, prior decisions will influence current decisions and the SEU model is no longer applicable. In exploring the characteristics of repeated decisions the following two conjectures guide the analysis:

1. When faced with repeated decisions of constant risk (allowing for end-game strategies), the time series of individuals' responses is stationary.
2. There is a significant correlation between current decisions and past decisions.

Following the lead of expected utility (and for that matter most, if not all, decision models) that individuals should treat decisions of similar risk consistently, the first conjecture suggests the consistency of the decision series. Without specifying the nature of an individual's utility function, this reduces to examining whether an individual's repeated decisions can be described as offering a stationary decision focus. In contrast, however, to the purely forward looking nature of expected utility, the second conjecture suggests that the repeated decisions of individuals are influenced by past decisions. The analysis will also consider the detailed nature of the trading strategies adopted. The characteristics of successful, in terms of net wealth generation, trading strategies also form part of the research agenda.

4. Specifics of the experimental design

By adopting an experimental approach, a number of problems that commonly plague the analysis of empirical data can be avoided. With respect to the general strengths of an experimental approach to analysis, Roth (1990), Smith (1991) and Hey (1991) all give excellent expositions. For a detailed exposition of the experimental design adopted in this study, reference should be made to Chapter 2. Also contained in Chapter 2 is a general discussion of potential design concerns. Therefore, this section only concerns itself with specific issues of the design as they relate directly to an analysis of repeated financial decisions and successful trading strategies.

At its most general, the trading behaviour of individuals should be derived in an environment where there are many commodities/shares. Thus, a criticism of the design might be an absence of a general portfolio of stocks from which to trade. This is, of course, difficult to operationalise experimentally (see Kroll *et al*, 1988a, b for experiments with two and three risky assets). Owing to the degree of complexity arising from the extended decision horizon in the current study and as a result of the obvious need to maintain a certain degree of simplicity, the experimental design adopted here only allows participants to substitute the riskless asset cash for the one traded share. Thus, there is no portfolio of risky assets that individuals are able to hold. The exact impact of this feature of the experiment on trading behaviour is difficult to determine a priori. One possible consequence is that trading may be biased downwards because of the lack of close substitutes. In contrast, with only a single share being available, trading may be increased because attention is focused solely on the given share. Given that the intention here is to analyse the decision processes individuals adopt in the light of repeated financial decisions, the absolute level of trade in a share, and associated potential bias, is of little concern. Of greater interest to the current study is an individual's decision to buy or sell in response to the given price.

The experiment might be argued to be unrealistic because the size and direction of trades have no impact on the next market price faced. This reflects, however, the atomistic price-taking framework at the heart of competitive financial markets. Hence, the price series is exogenous and there is no link between the actions of agents and the price series. Similarly, the experiment might be accused of creating an environment where traders never trade with others (or anybody). As before, however, this reflects the atomistic nature of financial markets: neither personalities nor reputations enter the trading process; individual agents simply buy/sell at the given market price. It is important to note also that if participants were able to affect the price series they face by their trades, then a great degree of experimental control would be lost.

A further conscious simplification is the zero return on the riskless asset cash. Again, given the research is concerned with the nature of trading behaviour rather than with the absolute level of trading, it is not clear how a zero return to the riskless asset would bias the results. Individuals were confronted with a series of difficult decisions under uncertainty and a conscious attempt was made to allow the participants to focus on the implicit risk and return characteristics of the tradable stock. It is difficult to see how the results would be affected by a zero rate of return as compared with the present real rate of return of 2%–3%. For these reasons and because of its simplicity, a zero rate of return was chosen for the riskless asset.

With the exception of the notional transaction cost of a 3-second time delay when an individual chooses to move the price series on without a decision to buy or sell having been made, there is an absence of transaction costs. There is no doubt that an absence of transaction costs can only have increased the propensity to trade. However, it must once more be remembered that absolute levels of trade were not a focus of concern in the current study. Given the presence of differing transaction costs in stock markets across the globe it was consciously decided to have no real transaction costs in the present analysis and thus establish one fixed point in the range of possibilities.

To maintain a reasonable sample size, participants were given the freedom to choose what time they attended the experiment on a given day. In addition, the computer cluster available to us across the five days had a maximum of 24 places at any one time. This means of ensuring a sufficient sample size (confounded by timetable logistics of the participants) and meeting the size constraint of the available computer cluster ran the risk of early participants informing later participants of the nature of the price series to be faced that day. None the less, whilst this potential cannot be denied, we conclude the risk of collusion to be minimal. A number of justifications for this conclusion are included in the discussion in Chapter 2.

Finally, it could be argued that a prize of £100 would have the consequence of inducing extreme trading behaviour due to tournament effects, generating a bias in the results. Whether the inclusion of a prize would result in more aggressive or more cautious trading behaviour than would otherwise have been observed is unclear. Certain participants may have become more risk-seeking in an attempt to win the prize. However, others may have adopted a more cautious approach so that their profit level increased steadily over the five days, thus negating the possibility that one erroneous trade would wipe out all the good work done in previous days. Whilst this type of effect would undoubtedly bias the results, such behaviour should have been reduced by the fact that the participants were not fully aware of their relative trading performance. As the experiment was run via open sessions across the whole of five days, it was difficult for the participants to assess relative performance at any one point in time. Furthermore, the selection of the participants from a broad range of departments across campus should have hampered comparison via personal discussion.

A fundamental criticism of experiments in economics focuses on their simplicity. Experiments are too simple to describe the real world, which is a far more complex phenomenon. Owing to their simplicity, experiments are artificial and abstract from reality. It is possible, therefore, to suggest that individuals will behave differently in the real world. Hey (1991, p. 13) 'counters this by arguing that, in experiments, the subjects (who are undoubtedly real) are tackling a real problem for real money, that their payment depends on their decisions and that everything about it is real'. Thus, the claim that experiments are not real is countered by having participants tackle a real (but stripped down) decision situation for real money. It must be acknowledged that the decision environment faced by participants is a simplification of the one faced by real investors. This, however, should be seen as a strength rather than a weakness. The simplicity allows the analysis to focus solely on the nature of individuals' decision processes in response to a series of prices without confounding factors (such as external shocks and liquidity effects) clouding the issue.

5. Analysis and results

Descriptive statistics

To form a backcloth to the main body of results, Table 3.1 summarises the relevant descriptive statistics for the practise session and the five days of trading. The first row

Table 3.1 Descriptive data

Row		Practise session	Days				
			1	2	3	4	5
1	Total number of decisions	2 101	23 154	31 377	35 200	41 453	47 872
2	To buy share decisions	645	6 746	9 102	10 104	11 022	14 782
3	To sell share decisions	686	7 552	11 303	12 758	18 127	21 567
4	To see next price decisions	680	8 856	10 972	12 338	12 304	11 523
	Price data (pence)						
5	Max price	345	371	229	675	492	635
6	Min price	296	236	98	160	324	360
7	Price range	49	135	131	515	168	275
8	Std. dev. price	1.41	3.74	3.60	15.03	4.90	6.00
9	Mean price	322	304	168	513	408	498
	Share data per decision						
10	Max shares	127	147	251	144	147	170
11	Min shares	0	0	0	0	0	0
12	Share range	127	147	251	144	147	170
13	Std. Dev. shares	17.89	17.66	28.05	22.32	14.70	12.17
14	Mean shares	74	45	83	56	61	57

of the table indicates that the number of trading decisions made by the 62 participants increased from 23 154 on day 1 to 47 872 on day 5. Thus, the analysis of the nature of the trading behaviour of individuals is derived from 179 056 trading decisions. Not surprisingly, a comparison of the number of decisions made each day in Table 3.1 indicates that as the participants became increasingly familiar/confident with the trading environment, their willingness to trade increased. Rows 5–9 of the table summarise the nature of the price series used in the experiment and they show that the price series are quite different for the various days of the experiment. For example, rows 5–8 indicate that the price series had quite different ranges and variances, whereas row 9 shows they also had differing mean levels of prices. The data on the shares traded per decision shown in the second half of Table 3.1 (rows 10–14) support the conclusion that the various days of trading were different and were perceived to be such by the participants. In other words, the conclusions to be drawn from the experimental data should be seen as being robust to differing forms of price series.

Repeated decision making

Before the specified conjectures are examined via the time series analysis of the individuals' buy/sell decisions, the properties of the underlying price series need to be considered. Of direct interest is whether the price series for each of the days is stationary. This is established by viewing the autocorrelation coefficients of the price series and by applying the Augmented Dickey–Fuller (unit root) test for stationarity. The Augmented Dickey–Fuller (ADF) test is based on the following. Consider the stochastic process:

$$\Delta z_t = \delta z_{t-1} + \varepsilon,$$

where Δ is the difference operator $z_t - z_{t-1}$; δ is $(\rho - 1)$; and ε is the normally distributed random error term.

The ADF test establishes whether $\delta = 0$ (that is, the autocorrelation coefficient $\rho = 1$). If the null hypothesis $\rho = 1$ is rejected, the time-series process is *stationary*. The ADF test statistic is $\tau = \rho/SE(\rho)$ with the critical rejection values being given by the MacKinnon tables.[5] Table 3.2 signifies the stationarity of the five price series used in the analysis via the application of the ADF test. As can be seen from the table, with a MacKinnon statistic of 2.8 for a 5% significance level and the still very high values of ρ at $k = 25$, the experimental price series data can be classed as non-stationary.

The stationarity of stochastic trading processes Having shown the price series faced by participants to be non-stationary processes, the stationarity of the time series of the participants' decision responses is considered. Letting each participant's responses to changes in share price over time be modelled as a stochastic process, such that each observation z_t is the proportion of the participant's cash stock converted to shares or the proportion of the participant's share stock converted to cash,[6] Tables 1–5 of Appendix II summarise the autocorrelation coefficients of the participants' decisions for the five days of the experiment, respectively. The decisions of the 62 participants over the five days provided a gross total of 310 decision time series. Given that short time-series realisations (less than 50 decision data points)[7] might not be reliable for computing autocorrelation coefficients with lags of up to 25, the net sample size reduces to 227 time-series realisations. Columns 1–11 of Tables

Table 3.2 Autocorrelation coefficients (e) of price series data

Day	Company	ADF 2.9@5%	Av.	1	2	3	4	Lag k 5	10	15	20	25
1	Al. Lyons	−1.84	578	1	1	1	0.99	0.99	0.98	0.97	0.96	0.95
2	Argyle	−1.21	302	1	1	1	1	0.99	0.99	0.98	0.97	0.96
3	Cadbury	−1.78	407	1	1	1	1	1	1	0.99	0.99	0.99
4	Coats	−1.48	165	1	1	1	1	0.99	0.99	0.98	0.97	0.97
5	Guinness	−1.90	498	1	1	1	1	1	1	1	1	1

1–5 of Appendix II show, respectively, the participant identification number (ID), the number (n) of decisions made by the participant on the day and the autocorrelation coefficients (ρ) for lags 1–25. For example, in Table 1 of Appendix II, the ID 2 row indicates that participant number 2 made 51 decisions to buy or sell various quantities of Allied Lyons stock.

The ADF test described above is used to determine whether the processes are stationary or non-stationary. The ADF statistics are shown in column 12 of the tables in Appendix II, the appearance of an S in column 13 indicating that the ADF test shows a root significantly less than one at the 5% level. From the application of the ADF test, 81% of the 227 decision series are stationary processes for lags up to 25 periods. The exceptions are as follows.

Day	ID	Total	Possible
1	14, 28, 34, 42, 60	5	42
2	4, 7, 11, 19, 20, 27, 34, 35, 37, 40, 43, 50, 52, 53, 54, 58	16	40
3	4, 7, 23, 25, 34	5	46
4	4, 7, 19, 31, 39, 43, 48	7	46
5	7, 15, 19, 25, 31, 34, 41, 43, 49	9	57

In contrast to the preliminary results of the pilot study (Ansic and Keasey, 1994) to the present analysis, the current results offer fairly strong evidence of individuals undertaking stationary (consistent) decision strategies. The result is noteworthy given the non-stationary nature of the underlying price series. Individuals seem to develop decision strategies that are reasonably immune to changes in the underlying series. The implications of such consistency/fixedness for the modelling of decisions and markets are considered in the concluding section.

The 19% of the participant sample shown to be non-stationary can now be accounted for by differencing the first-difference decision time series. The methodology required to establish whether a process is integrated is described by Gujarati (1995, pp. 721–4). The original first-difference regressions ($\Delta \tilde{z}_t = z_t - z_{t-1}$) on z_{t-1} are now differenced again to give

$$\Delta \tilde{D}_t = \Delta z_t - \Delta z_{t-1} = z_t - 2z_{t-1} + z_{t-2},$$

which are regressed on

$$D_{t-1} = \Delta z_{t-1} = z_{t-1} - z_{t-2}.$$

The ADF t-scores for the regressions are listed in column 14 of Tables 1–5 of Appendix II. The MacKinnon critical t-value is 2.89 at the 5% level and the appearance of an S in column 15 indicates that the coefficient on D_{t-1} is a root significantly less than one. That is, the process is stationary. It can be concluded, therefore, that Δz_t is stationary and an Integrated I(1) process. Every one of the

227 sample realisations can, therefore, be classified as stationary at this level of differencing.

With reference to the second conjecture stated above, the evidence discussed in the previous subsection indicates that individuals adopt stationary decision strategies where current decisions are related to prior decisions. Visual inspection of the autocorrelation functions suggests that approximately 77% of decision processes could be classified as being either $AR(p)$ or $ARMA(p, q)$, thus including some autoregressive component. The dominant strategic form was, therefore, of an autoregressive nature. The most general conclusion to be drawn is that current decisions are related to prior decisions. Further light can be thrown on the nature of these decision series via an analysis of the nature of the trading strategies.

In summary, from the evidence of the decision time series, the current results suggest that individuals adopt largely consistent decision strategies in the context of repeated decisions. Furthermore, such consistency is apparent even when the decision makers face non-stationary price series.

The characteristics of successful trading strategies   Taking each trader decision day as the unit of analysis, a runs test (see Appendix III for description) was used to identify significant (at the 5% level) patterns of trading behaviour. The outcomes of this analysis are summarised in Tables 3.3 and 3.4. The analysis indicated that the trading strategies could be categorised into two basic types, a 'buyer's' strategy and a 'seller's' strategy. The definitions adopted here are as follows. A buyer's strategy consists of lots of small buy decisions followed by a large sell decision. In contrast, a seller's strategy consists of lots of small sell decisions followed by a large buy decision. Thus, although these two strategies are equally asymmetric, and this is important in itself, they work from a different basic stance. The buying strategy works from primarily holding cash and then slowly converting the inventory of cash into a holding of a share, whereas a seller's strategy consists of primarily holding an inventory of a share and then slowly converting it into cash. Tables 3.3 and 3.4 respectively summarise, via a common format, the data for the buyer's strategy and the seller's strategy.

The data summarised in Tables 3.3 and 3.4 refer to those decision days for which a significant (at the 5% level) runs test was obtained. Hence, from a maximum number of 310 (5 days times 62 participants) decision days, Tables 3.3 and 3.4 in total cover 238 decision days—the other 72 decision days consisted of mixed (not consistent) trading strategies that, incidentally, earned considerably less than the buyer's or seller's strategies. However, the categories of best to worst of each table were determined on the basis of all decision days. Hence, for a given day of the experiment the distribution of earnings for all individuals was allocated to the quartiles of best to worst. From this basis, if on a given day an individual's earnings were in the top quartile and if his strategy could be defined as a buyer's, then there would be one observation in the best category of Table 3.3. Thus, from column 10 of Table 3.3, of the 120 decision days that could be clearly characterised as a buyer's strategy, 19 were from the top quartile of earnings for any given day, 35 were from the second quartile, 36 from the third quartile and 30 from the bottom quartile of the distribution. A similar interpretation can be made of Table 3.4.

Table 3.3 Significant runs test group ($Z > 1.96$) using a buyer's strategy

	No. of buy decisions	No. of sell decisions	Volume of shares bought	Volume of shares sold	Ratio of the no. of buy:sell decisions	Volume traded on BUY decisions	Volume traded on SELL decisions	Av. yield for (5 days)	Yield std. dev. (5 days)	Person-days
	1	2	3	4	5	6	7	8	9	10
Best	474	244	2797	2832	1.94	5.90	11.61	532.68	173.57	19
Good	324	244	1941	1978	1.33	5.99	8.11	488.86	137.05	35
Fair	294	199	2380	2428	1.48	8.10	12.20	465.97	110.47	36
Worst	279	190	1986	2004	1.47	7.12	10.55	422.47	117.84	30
										120

Table 3.4 Significant runs test group ($Z > 1.96$) using a seller's strategy

	No. of buy decisions	No. of sell decisions	Volume of shares bought	Volume of shares sold	Ratio of the no. of sell:buy decisions	Volume traded on BUY decisions	Volume traded on SELL decisions	Av. yield for (5 days)	Yield std. dev. (5 days)	Person-days
	1	2	3	4	5	6	7	8	9	10
Best	211	904	3434	3435	4.28	16.27	3.80	642.54	214.98	24
Good	230	386	1794	1841	1.68	7.80	4.77	519.15	160.57	47
Fair	255	332	1646	1686	1.48	7.32	5.08	475.75	107.04	12
Worst	190	346	1782	1833	1.82	9.38	5.30	462.67	140.41	35
										118

Columns 1 and 2 of Tables 3.3 and 3.4 indicate the number of buy and sell decisions. Not surprisingly, the buy strategies of Table 3.3 have significantly more buys than sells, whereas the sell strategies of Table 3.4 have significantly more sells than buys. However, more importantly, it is clear from Table 3.3 that the best buy strategies make significantly more buy decisions than the other categories of good to worst, although they do not make significantly more sell decisions. This is also evident from the buy/sell ratio of column 5 of Table 3.3. Similarly, the best of the seller's strategies make significantly more sell decisions than the good to worst categories but no more buy decisions. Hence, it is clear that the most successful of these asymmetric strategies is extremely active on one side of the decision-making process; namely, the most successful of the buyer's strategies actively make a lot of buy decisions and the most successful of the seller's strategies actively make a lot of sell decisions.

Columns 3, 4, 6 and 7 of Tables 3.3 and 3.4 provide data on the volume of shares traded. For both buyer and seller strategies, it is evident from columns 3 and 4 that the best category traded more total volume on both sides of the transaction than the other categories. In terms of the buyer's strategy of Table 3.3, columns 6 and 7 indicate that the best group did not buy more volume per decision than the other groups but, in general, it did sell a marginally larger volume per decision than the other groups. Hence, for the buyer's strategy, success seems to be more a function of activity (the number of decisions made) than aggression (the volume of shares traded per decision). In contrast, success with the seller's strategy does seem to be a function of aggression as well as activity. Column 6 of Table 3.4 indicates that the best group was far more willing to take an 'exposed' position in terms of the volume of shares it bought per decision. In other words, the best of the seller's strategy were willing to take the risk of holding a larger inventory of the shares. Interestingly, the best group made a lot more smaller sell decisions than the other groups (see columns 2 and 7 of Table 3.4). Thus, for the buyer's strategy there is evidence that success is a function of activity and to a lesser degree aggression. Whereas, for the seller's strategy, success would seem to be a function of both activity and aggression.

The above results raise the questions why individuals adopt asymmetric strategies and why success is a function of the strategies being played actively and aggressively. First and foremost, an asymmetric strategy that emphasises one side of the transaction considerably eases decision making within a repeated decision environment. For example, with a seller's strategy the purchase of a large block of a share at price £X per unit allows the trader to concentrate on following the simple rule of 'sell so long as price is above £X per unit'. Of course, if there is a belief that prices are rising, then the trader will only sell a part of his/her inventory of a share in the hope that the remainder will be sold at higher prices. In contrast, if the trader bought a share at a range of prices, it would become increasingly difficult to keep track of whether profits or losses are being made on sales. Similarly, the simplicity of being able to concentrate on a single price of purchase allows the trader to be more active in the number of decisions made and be more confident that profits are being gained; hence, the tendency for successful individuals to be more active and aggressive in their trading. The asymmetric buying strategy follows a similar type of logic. Here, the emphasis, however, is towards buying on trends of prices. If small parcels of a share are bought at different points of a rising trend, then the trader only needs to compare, assuming a smoothness in price changes, the latest price with the previous price to know if a profit is to be made on all the inventory of the share. Again, the simplicity of trading introduced by the asymmetric rule allows traders to pursue success via activity and, to a lesser extent, aggression. Asymmetry, activity and aggression are the 3As of successful trading.

Finally, if Tables 3.3 and 3.4 are compared, it is evident from column 8 that the seller's strategy earned more than the buyer's strategy. This can be explained in the following way. The seller's strategy is inherently more risky than the buyer's because its primary holding is in a share rather than cash and it is, therefore, exposed to substantial gains on price rises and substantial losses on price falls. It so happens that the price series used in the experiment exhibited general, but marginal, increases; hence, the greater gains made by the seller's strategy.

6. Discussion and conclusions

The purpose of this chapter has been to analyse repeated decision making in the context of financial trading decisions. After a brief introduction, the study discussed the differences between unique and repeated decisions. Section 3 drew on existing literature as a means of positioning the current study. The existing literature was also used to develop tentative conjectures concerning repeated decision making. A consideration of specific experimental design issues followed, before Section 5 embarked on a detailed analysis of the data. In essence, the experiment involved recording the trading (buy/sell) responses of 62 individuals to the price series of five different stocks across five days of trading. From analysis of the data three conclusions can be drawn. First, even in the face of non-stationary price series, individuals adopt stationary (consistent) decision series. That is, when confronted with shifting distributions of prices, individuals adopt reasonably firm decision strategies. Secondly, these strategies are such that decisions across time are related, with current decisions being most influenced by the more recent decisions. Hence, in a repeated decision context, individual decisions are not seen as isolated one-off events but rather are dealt with as being part of a series of such decisions (contrary to Kroll *et al* 1988a, b). Given the costs of dealing with such a decision context, it is perhaps not surprising that individuals seem to adopt decision strategies that minimise on information and 'decision' costs. Thirdly, the exploratory analysis also considered, via the use of runs tests, whether the decision series of the individuals displayed consistently recognisable, systematic patterns of behaviour. Two basic trading patterns emerged: a seller's strategy where an individual bought a large inventory of a share at a given price and then sold small parcels of the share from the inventory, and a buyer's strategy where the individual primarily held wealth as cash and then slowly bought small parcels of the share. The successful trading emanating from these two asymmetric strategies had two salient characteristics—activity and aggression. The successful traders used the simplicity of focus of the strategies to make a lot more decisions and trade more volume. Thus, successful active trading within a repeated decision context has three features—asymmetry, activity and aggression—the 3As of successful trading.

Given the above results and conclusions, two issues to be considered are how such decision behaviour might affect the modelling of decisions and the operation of markets. In terms of modelling decisions, the present results clearly indicate that within the context of repeated decisions under uncertainty, individuals seem to adopt decision strategies that economise on the obvious decision and information costs via heuristics that make use of past decisions and that focus on one aspect (buy or sell) of transactions. In addition, the costs of repeated decision making will be reduced by the continued use of a particular decision strategy. In essence, individuals in the present context minimise on decision costs by focusing on one side of the decision; that is, they adopt buy or sell strategies. The results suggest, therefore, that repeated decisions may not be treated as isolated one-off events that can be handled with a purely forward looking mentality but rather decision makers cope with the high decision and information costs of repeated decision making under uncertainty via strategies that make use of past decisions. In terms of the impact of the current results on the behaviour of markets, at the most obvious level the stationary responses of individuals to non-stationary price series should have the beneficial effect of lending stability to markets. However, given the use of past decisions within the noted decision processes, the obvious benefits of stability might be replaced by the less attractive characteristic of market 'stickiness'; that is, where there is a slow response to changes in market parameters. Whether the noted decision processes lead to stability or stickiness, and this will ultimately depend on the exact characteristics of the particular market of interest, it is possible that the success associated with asymmetric decision strategies (either focusing on the sell or buy side of market transactions) might be one explanation of the cyclical nature of many markets. In general, therefore, further research could usefully explore how the characteristics of repeated decision making discussed here might be used to explain the commonly noted market features of hysteresis and cycles.

4 Do the demand curves for stocks slope downwards?

1. Introduction

The nature of the decision process and the choice of trading strategy adopted by individuals, in aggregate, have direct implications for the demand function faced by the traded security. Much of finance theory is based on the premise that the demand curve for stocks is highly price-elastic (or horizontal in the extreme). Thus, the determination of the type of demand function faced by financial stocks is of paramount importance. Lynn Stout concludes her 1990 *Yale Law Journal* article on takeover premiums with the following quotation:

> The question of whether the demand for stocks is horizontal or downward sloping is far from answered. Additional theoretical development and empirical testing are necessary. But so long as assumptions concerning stock demand elasticity determine perspectives on appropriate regulation, the stakes are more than high enough to demand further inquiry (p. 1296).

This chapter is intended to complement the existing empirical literature on the demand function for financial securities via the adoption of an experimental approach. The issue is clearly important since a number of theorems of finance, as well as the calculation of takeover premiums, depend upon the demand curves for stocks being horizontal or highly price-elastic. For example, the active arbitrage mechanism that underpins the efficiency results of the finance literature depends upon a demand curve that is horizontal or displays a high degree of price-elasticity. The previous empirical literature has been unable to address directly the price–demand relationship due to confounding influences such as event and information effects. In an attempt to address strictly the price–demand relationship, the approach adopted here is to follow the lead of Fisher Black (1986) who notes:

> People sometimes trade on information in the usual way...On the other hand, people sometimes trade on noise as if it were information...noise trading is essential to the existence of liquid markets (p. 529).

It may well be a mistake to examine the demand curve for stocks with the implicit assumption of homogeneous traders and/or homogeneous trading. The notion of noisy trading is that individuals are actively buying/selling stocks on the basis of price movements alone with no other supporting information, whereas with informed trading, the trading decision is based on/supported by other information.

Notwithstanding the finer difficulties of precisely separating noise from information in the context of financial markets, the basic categorisation of noisy and informed traders can usefully illustrate how demand curves for stocks may differ across trader types. Focusing solely on the noise trader type ensures that quantities demanded are affected only by price changes, thus removing any confounding effects. Given Black's (1986) definitions of noise and informed trader types, it must be recognised that the former group of traders will generate a more price-elastic demand function than the latter. Thus, if a highly price-elastic demand function is not apparent in this most favourable of scenarios, with noise traders only, then it is highly questionable whether the demand functions faced by financial securities are highly price-elastic (horizontal) more generally. The structure of the remainder of the chapter is as follows. The following section introduces relevant empirical literature, discussing both the results and limitations of the studies. Section 3 argues that the limitations of conventional empirical studies can be overcome via the use of experimental methods. The section goes on to discuss specific issues of potential concern associated with the experimental design as they relate to an analysis of the demand function for financial stocks. Analysis and results are presented in Section 4 and Section 5 contains discussion and conclusions.

2. Empirical literature

The obvious benefit of utilising empirical approaches to examine the slope of the demand curve for stocks is that they use data generated by the real-world stock markets. For example, the early empirical tests of the slope of the demand curve for stocks consisted of analysing the price reactions to the large block sale (purchase) of stocks.[1] The analysis by Marsh (1979) of the response to rights issues in the UK is a good example of this type of approach. Marsh noted, in contrast to the US findings (for example, see footnote 1), that the demand curve for equities was highly price-elastic, with stocks suffering only a temporary marginal reduction in price when they went ex-rights. The general finding of downward sloping demand curves is, however, as noted by Shleifer (1986), confounded by potential information effects. In response to the weakness of the block sales test, Shleifer suggested a test based upon the inclusion of a firm's stock in the S&P500 index. Upon inclusion in the S&P500, a stock is argued to suffer an increase in demand as index and pension funds attempt to maintain their portfolios in line with this major index. If the demand curve for the stock is downward sloping, then such a shift in demand should lead to an increase in price, whereas if the demand curve is horizontal any shift in demand will have no effect upon price. By using an event study methodology on the returns of 246 firms for the period from 1966 to 1983, Shleifer found statistical and substantive support for the demand curves for stocks being downward sloping. This approach to testing the nature of the demand curve for stocks is not, however, without its own problems; for example, as Shleifer himself notes, the inclusion of a stock in an index may impart risk, information and liquidity effects as well as a pure shift in demand. In addition, it uses a response to a unique event, a change in the *ceteris paribus* conditions, to derive implications about the general nature of the demand curves for stocks. In other words, it uses the response of stock returns to being included in an index to draw implications concerning the relationship between the price and quantities of a stock under normal trading conditions. Thirdly, and related to the second point, the approach is able to say little about the price-elasticity of the demand curve for a stock, in that it can only conclude whether or not there has been a price effect.

3. Specifics of the experimental design

The fundamental flaw in the conventional empirical analysis is, therefore, the lack of control of external factors such that it is impossible to isolate the price–demand relationship. In contrast to the indirect empirical analysis, the experimental design utilised here has the advantage of offering a direct analysis of how the demand for a stock responds to changes in its price whilst holding other conditions constant. In other words, the demand responses to price changes are derived under *ceteris paribus* conditions. This type of analysis therefore avoids all the major hindrances associated with an empirical approach, as introduced above.

A common approach to experimentation in the financial literature has been to design small markets where less than a dozen individuals trade with each other for no more than an hour or two on the basis of artificially generated data. The tradition of these designs may in part be due to the problems of creating realistic financial markets that adequately embrace the essential market dynamics of many participants, real time, real stock price movements and massive database output. The present design departs from experimental design convention because the intention here is to attempt partially to account for some of these dynamics so as to study the nature of the demand curve for stocks. A further reason for the departure from convention is the large number of observations of the price-to-quantity-demanded relationship required in order to estimate the demand function. The small market designs typically generate too few observations at given price levels. The strength of the current design is the large number of observations (quantities demanded) generated for a given price.

An experimental design is not, however, by nature a perfect representation of reality and in Chapter 2 we discussed general criticisms of both the experimental approach and the specific design adopted in the current study. The discussion in this section will, therefore, concern itself only with specific issues of the experimental design and approach as they relate to the study of the demand function for financial securities.

To ensure that the participants were fully motivated to the best of their ability, we introduced a prize of £100 for the best performance over the week. It could be argued, however, that a final prize of £100 would have the consequence of inducing risk-seeking trading behaviour with a concomitant increase in the elasticity of the demand curve for stocks. In answer to this there are a number of points of note: first, given that the experiment consisted of individuals playing against a market, it is not clear that risk-seeking behaviour would be induced; secondly, even if risk-seeking behaviour were induced, it is not clear what risk-seeking behaviour would constitute within the context of the present dynamic environment (utility functions are normally defined in a static context) and thirdly, it is unclear how risk-seeking behaviour would impact upon the demand curve for stocks. In addition, it was argued in Chapter 2 that the introduction of a £100 prize may even have caused individuals to become more cautious when trading so as to ensure that one erroneous trade did not wipe out all the profit (and a chance of winning the prize) they had earned up to that point. The £100 prize was introduced to attract participants and to ensure they took the experiment seriously. It has to be recognised, however, that the introduction of such an incentive may have had unforeseen consequences for the eventual results. As argued above, any experimental design is a compromise.

One possible concern is that because the participants had no other information apart from prices on which to judge the stocks, this may have increased the elasticity of demand, the argument being that an absence of other information increases the uniformity of reservation prices across the participants and hence the elasticity of general demand for a given stock. Clearly, the very strength of the experimental approach is its ability to examine one factor while holding others constant. In the present context, the intention was to consider quantity responses to price changes, holding all other factors constant. This design was adopted because the introduction of other information may have potentially confounded the analysis of the responsiveness of demand to price changes. None the less, it has to be accepted that the current analysis is concerned with analysing the trading responses of noisy traders, rather than traders in general. As the dominant characteristic of noisy trading is that it places primary emphasis on price movements with little or no recognition of other factors, there is likely to be an upward bias in terms of the elasticity of the demand for stocks. On the face of it, this may be seen as a fundamental flaw of the experimental design. However, two responses are applicable. First, given Black's (1986) distinction between informed and noisy traders, it would be a mistake to treat traders as homogeneous and proceed to estimate an associated price-elasticity of demand. It would be more fruitful to recognise the existence of distinct trader types and estimate the price-elasticity of demand for each in isolation. The approach adopted, therefore, is to exploit the degree of control afforded by the experimental method and investigate the price-elasticity of demand associated with noisy traders, thus complementing the empirical work more suited to an investigation of the price-elasticity of demand associated with informed traders. Secondly, much of finance theory is premised on the assumption of the demand curve for stocks being horizontal or highly price-elastic. The analysis here can be seen to be giving the theory a 'best shot'. If a theory fails in an environment designed at giving it a best shot, then it will certainly fail in reality. Evidence indicating a price-inelastic demand for noisy traders would, therefore, be condemning evidence falsifying one of the underlying assumptions of finance theory.

A related criticism of the current experimental design is that an absence of a general portfolio of stocks from which to trade will have increased the elasticity of the demand for a single tradable stock in the experiment. In other words, at its most general, the demand curve for an individual stock should be derived in an environment where there are many stocks. The exact impact of this feature of the experiment on the demand curve for the stock is difficult to determine a priori. One possible consequence is that the price-elasticity of the demand for the stock may be biased upwards because attention is focused solely on the given stock. If this is indeed the case, then it is again possible to advocate the 'best shot' argument as illustrated above. It is, however, possible that the price-elasticity of demand will be biased downwards because of the lack of close substitutes. The exact nature of any bias is difficult to envisage a priori and could be investigated in future work.

Another potential criticism is that the absence of transaction costs (with the exception of a 3-second time delay for deciding not to do anything) within the experiment will have increased the elasticity of demand. There is no doubt that an absence of transaction costs can only have increased the propensity to trade. However, given the presence of differing transaction costs in stock markets across the globe and an absence of knowledge over the exact impact of transaction costs on trading behaviour, it was decided to have no real financial transaction costs in the present analysis since this establishes one fixed point in the range of possibilities. Future experimental work could usefully establish the impact of transaction costs on trading behaviour. Again, the design can be seen to be giving the theory a 'best shot' with respect to the assumption of a high price-elasticity of demand.

A further issue of concern may be that the riskless asset cash offers a zero rate of return and this may have increased the elasticity of demand for stocks. This was, however, part of an attempt to allow the participants to focus on the implicit risk and return characteristics of the tradable stock. From the price information available, individuals were confronted with a series of difficult decisions under uncertainty. It was felt that little would be gained by adding the complication of a return to the riskless asset. Furthermore, given the research is concerned with the slope of the demand curve for stocks rather than with the absolute level of demand, it is unclear how a zero return to the riskless asset would bias the results. In addition, it is difficult to see how the results would be affected by a zero rate of return as compared with the present real rate of return of 2% to 3%. It is for these reasons, and because of its simplicity, that a zero rate of return was chosen for the riskless asset.

In summary, the current experiment was designed to complement, as simply as possible, the existing empirical literature on the demand curve for stocks. The experiment aimed to capture the demand responses of active investors (noisy traders) within a dynamic trading environment, where participants were motivated to disclose their responses to the prices of a stock. Furthermore, by providing price series that differed in terms of their levels, ranges and degrees of volatility (see below), the experiment was designed to check the robustness of any perceived patterns of behaviour. An additional benefit of the experiment containing five days of trading was that it allowed the participants to become fully conversant with the general trading environment.

4. Analysis and results

The analysis and results of Chapter 3 have established that the participants in the experiment were pursuing increases in wealth via active trading strategies. This section now explores the nature of the demand curves for stocks. To this end, Figure 4.1 graphs the average demand for stocks at each price level observed by

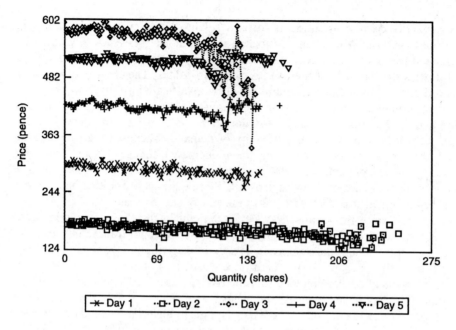

Figure 4.1 Average demand for shares

subjects over the five days of trading, where each observation of the quantity of stocks demanded is assumed to be a random variable with mean $\bar{S}_P$ at price P. Although the approach approximates the real world, where a specific price could occur many times across a given life of a market, it does suffer, on the face of it, from a shortcoming. The aggregation of stocks demanded for a specific price across the experiment[2] implies that different underlying conditions (different information sets) are also being aggregated and thus the strict *ceteris paribus* condition could be broken. It needs to be noted, however, that some form of aggregation was necessary because of the nature of the data (that is, a single price could have occurred many times) and, furthermore, only prices that were common to all participants were aggregated. A commonality of prices was achieved by deleting those 'outlying' price observations only achieved by students who progressed particularly quickly (this explains the reduction in observations between Tables 3.1 and 4.1).

Considering the graphs of Figure 4.1, both individually and together, there is clear evidence that the demand curves for stocks are highly price-elastic. Even after allowing for any scaling influences, it is quite apparent from the graphs themselves that there is strong positive support for the hypothesis that the demand curves for stocks are highly price-elastic.

The graphs also indicate that the relationships between prices and quantities are highly linear but suffer mild heteroscedasticity and possible changes in functional form towards the upper end of the quantity range. The graphs seem to indicate, therefore, that the behaviour of the participants changes when faced with extreme trading situations.[3] In other words, trading behaviour is consistent across a wide range of quantities but becomes excessively 'noisy' at the positive extreme of the quantity distribution.

The small sample of noisy data causes a number of difficulties for the econometric analysis of the general dataset; for example, a Spearman Rank test of the squared residuals indicates the presence of heteroscedasticity. Two approaches are taken in this chapter to deal with this issue: first, the overall data set is transformed to cope

Table 4.1 Regression results

		Days				
		1	2	3	4	5
Intercept	Unadjust	303.653	180.417	587.584	429.346	524.216
	Transform	302.772	175.539	578.609	424.909	523.564
	Truncate	303.412	179.656	584.167	427.735	521.205
Slope	Unadjust	−0.169	−0.126	−0.280	−0.197	−0.145
	Transform	−0.138	−0.031	−0.089	−0.077	−0.126
	Truncate	−0.161	−0.119	−0.174	−0.144	−0.047
Observation	Unadjust	19 676(136)	28 161(123)	29 864(129)	36 085(137)	42 503(148)
	Transform	136	123	129	137	148
	Truncate	16 161(100)	15 956(100)	25 737(100)	25 294(100)	33 306(100)
$\bar{R}^2$	Unadjust	0.5112	0.6129	0.4124	0.4689	0.2171
	Transform	0.9998	0.9998	0.9999	0.9999	0.9999
	Truncate	0.3387	0.3900	0.3218	0.4196	0.0859
F-Test	Unadjust	20 575	44 582	20 961	31 851	11 789
		(0.0000)	(0.0000)	(0.0000)	(0.0000)	(0.0000)
	Transform	2 774 274	953 655	4 435 206	5 188 730	8 094 036
		(0.0000)	(0.0000)	(0.0000)	(0.0000)	(0.0000)
	Truncate	8 275	10 201	12 213	18 283	3 131
		(0.0000)	(0.0000)	(0.0000)	(0.0000)	(0.0000)
Functional form	Unadjust	0.7	5.3	56.6	20.2	13.2
	Transform	1.5	4.7	21.9	1.0	1.1
	Truncate	0.1	0.1	2.0	0.3	0.5
Normality	Unadjust	18.9	10.8	311.1	628.7	135.5
	Transform	6.3	13.4	149.2	122.3	40.1
	Truncate	3.4	47.3	3.5	0.9	4.8
Hetero-scedasticity	Unadjust	3.6	5.5	16.0	5.6	14.6
	Transform	0.9	0.1	0.7	0.1	2.0
	Truncate	0.1	2.2	0.0	0.5	3.0

Note:
Functional form = Ramsey's RESET test using the square of the fitted values, chi-squared values given for one degree of freedom.
Normality = Based on a test of skewness and kurtosis residuals, chi-squared values given for two degrees of freedom.
Heteroscedasticity = Based on the regression of squared residuals on squared fitted values, chi-squared values given for one degree of freedom.
Chi-squared values at the 95% confidence level for one and two degrees of freedom are 3.841 and 5.991, respectively.

with the problems caused by the sample of extreme observations; secondly, the data set is truncated to exclude the extreme observations. Clearly, both approaches have their shortcomings. As the results will indicate, although the transformations of the first approach deal directly with the heteroscedasticity problems created by the extreme observations, the transformations lead to other issues of concern. Similarly, by truncating the data set, valuable data is being lost. For these reasons, three sets of regression results are presented—unadjusted, transformed and truncated regressions (see Table 4.1). For the unadjusted and truncated regressions, weighted average regressions (where the quantity means for each price class are weighted by the number of quantity observations in each price class) are performed to allow for different price classes not having the same number of quantity observations. For example, Table 4.1 shows that for the unadjusted regression for day 1, there were 19 676 quantity observations across 136 price classes (see parentheses). For the transformed regressions this effect is allowed for by the nature of the transformation itself. The data suggested that an appropriate transformation for heteroscedasticity would consist of dividing through the overall function by the average demand for stocks at each class price (independent variable).[4] Finally, the aggregate data sets for each of the days of trading were truncated down to 100 observations so as to avoid the noisy samples of data at the upper ends of the distributions. Comparison of these three sets of regressions (undertaken within SPSS) should give a full impression of the robustness of the achieved results.

It is readily apparent from the F statistics of Table 4.1 that the intercept and slope coefficients for all three forms of regressions are highly statistically significant for each of the days of trading. Moreover, if attention is directed towards the diagnostic statistics presented in Table 4.1, then it is quite clear that the truncated regression is generally the best specified of the three—having residuals that are normally distributed around a mean of zero and, generally, homoscedastic. Furthermore, with the exception of day 5, the $\bar{R}^2$s indicate that the truncated regressions explain an acceptable level of variance within the dependent variable.[5] From the truncated regressions, as well as for the other regressions, it is apparent that the slope coefficients are highly price-elastic.

Thus, the graphs and the regression results offer strong positive support for the premise that the demand curves for stocks of noisy traders are highly price-elastic.

5. Discussion and conclusions

From a base of 179 056 decisions across a number of different price series on five trading days, the experimental evidence presented here suggests the demand curves for stocks of noisy traders are highly price-elastic. In contrast, prior empirical studies have generally found demand curves for stocks to be downward sloping. The question that remains is how to view these two differing sets of results. One approach, but not the one taken here, would be to argue for the relative merits of a particular methodology and then take the related results as being generally indicative. Another approach, and the one taken here, is to consider how different methodologies complement one another to illuminate an issue from differing perspectives.

The analyses to date have assumed that trading within financial markets is homogeneous but as Fisher Black (1986) notes,

> People sometimes trade on information in the usual way ... On the other hand, people sometimes trade on noise as if it were information ... noise trading is essential to the existence of liquid markets (p. 529).

In other words, we may well be mistaken to examine the demand curve for stocks with the implicit assumption of homogeneous traders and/or homogeneous trading. To consider the implications of this, Black's noisy and informed trading categorisation was used as a starting point. The notion of noisy trading is that individuals are actively buying/selling stocks on the basis of price movements alone with no other supporting information, whereas with informed trading, the trading decision is based on/supported by other information. Notwithstanding the finer difficulties of precisely separating noise from information in the context of financial markets, the basic categorisation of noisy and informed traders can usefully illustrate how demand curves for stocks may differ and how different methodologies might be used to analyse them. Considering the elasticity of demand curves first, there is a good reason why noisy traders may have more elastic curves than informed traders. By their very nature, noisy traders focus on prices alone and hence they should be sensitive to price movements. In contrast, informed traders judge price movements in a wider context and they should, therefore, be expected to be less sensitive to price movements than noisy traders.

Having considered how noisy and informed traders may have differing elasticities of demand for stocks, there is now a need to reflect on the types of analysis that might be suitable for retrieving these elasticities from trading behaviour. The dominant characteristic of noisy trading is that it places primary emphasis on price movements with little or no recognition of other factors. The current experiment was designed to analyse exactly this form of trading and retrieve the related elasticities. In contrast, prior empirical work with its emphasis on the response of the demand for stocks to events, seems far more suited to retrieving the elasticities of demand of informed trading. In other words, it should come as no surprise that the current experimental and prior empirical analyses of the demand for stocks have given different impressions of the elasticities of the demand for stocks, for they have essentially analysed different types of trading behaviour. In that the two forms of analysis are able, and have been used, to tackle different types of trading behaviour within financial markets, they should be seen as complementary.

In conclusion, this chapter has analysed the experimental data generated by the general design adopted here and offers evidence that complements the existing empirical literature on the demand curve for stocks. It finds that active (noisy) trading behaviour gives rise to highly elastic demand curves. Thus, although the decision-making framework that individuals seem to adopt in the context of repeated financial decisions (that is, based on past prices and asymmetric in outlook) is somewhat different from that proposed in finance theory, one of the key outcomes of such behaviour—an elastic demand curve for stocks—is identical to that assumed by finance theory. This suggests, to us at least, that finance theory might usefully explore the implications of richer decision models. It is not apparent that the whole edifice of finance theory need crumble and, indeed, further insights might be gained by considering how different decision models (for example, asymmetric buy-and-sell trading strategies) might come together to create financial markets. In fact, some of the more obvious phenomena of financial markets—at times volatile, cyclical and sticky—might begin to be understood if we move away from viewing market participants as always responding with a symmetric and purely future-looking perspective.

5 Repeated financial decisions and the leptokurtic nature of stock distributions

1. Introduction

The common feature linking the previous chapters is their focus on repeated financial decision making and, more specifically, the identification of the nature and defining characteristics of repeated decisions. This chapter will continue this theme by discussing the possible implications for observed portfolio returns and price/return distributions. Chapter 3 reports that successful repeated decisions can be characterised as stationary decision processes that adhere to the 3As of trading—asymmetry, activity and aggression. The discussion to follow will link these defining characteristics with the empirically reported leptokurtism of stock returns (for example, see Fama, 1965; Affleck-Graves and McDonald, 1989; Richardson and Smith, 1993). Section 2 discusses the importance and implications for the finance literature of price/return distributions and comments on empirical findings in this area. The section also offers a conjecture that the nature of repeated financial decisions may in some way be responsible for leptokurtic returns. Section 3 concerns experimental design and method considerations and limitations of the current study. Indirect analysis and results pertaining to the conjecture are reported in Section 4, while the final section contains discussion and tentative conclusions.

2. Finance theory, price/return distributions and a conjecture

Much of mainstream finance theory is premised on the building blocks of risk and return. By definition, when appraising a risky investment the future return will not be known with certainty, there will be a range (or distribution) of possible returns. The convention in the finance literature is to adopt the expected return ($E(r)$) as the expression of an investment's return and the standard deviation of returns (σ) as the measure of risk involved. It is generally accepted that any investment proposal can be appraised on the basis of these two measures alone. Indeed, from Equation (1) below:

$$E[U(r)] = a + bE(r) - c\sigma^2 + cE(r)^2 \qquad (1)$$

it is clear that the expected utility produced by an investment is determined by the three individual-specific, risk-attitude constants (a, b, c) and the expected return ($E(r)$) and the variance of returns (σ^2). (See Lumby, 1991, for a detailed exposition.)

The importance of the two measures, expected return and standard deviation of return, to finance theory is now discussed with reference to two fundamental theories. Portfolio theory, and the notion of diversification, is built around the measures $E(r)$ and σ. A portfolio of shares that are not perfectly, positively correlated will have an expected return based on the weighted average return of the shares in the portfolio, but the risk of the portfolio will be *less than* the weighted average of the risk of the individual shares. The degree to which diversification permits a reduction in risk is based on the correlation of returns of all shares that make up the portfolio. The farther away from perfect, positive correlation are the returns, the greater the benefits from diversification. The capital asset pricing model (CAPM) is the second fundamental finance technique founded on the use of $E(r)$ and σ. In the world of the CAPM it is assumed that investors hold a fully diversified portfolio of shares and thus they are only rewarded for exposure to systematic risk. The expected return on a given security is calculated thus:

$$E(r_i) = r_f + (r_m - r_f)\beta_i, \tag{2}$$

where $E(r_i)$ is the expected return on security i, r_f is the return on the risk free asset, r_m is the return on the market portfolio and $\beta_i = \mathrm{cov}(r_i, r_m)/\sigma_m^2$ is the relative measure of the risk of security i. If r_f and r_m are given, then the sole determinant of an individual share's $E(r_i)$ is the value of β_i. Thus, the two measures $E(r)$ and σ both underpin the workings of the CAPM.

Imperative to finance theory, then, is the ability adequately to describe the distribution of returns by reference to a measure of central tendency, $E(r)$, and a measure of the dispersion of returns around this central tendency, σ. This is acceptable if the returns are normally distributed. However, if returns are not normally distributed then $E(r)$ and σ are no longer sufficient fully to describe the nature of the returns distribution and additional measures are required, including the degree of skew and kurtosis.

The foundations of finance are therefore built on the assumption that returns are normally distributed and that a knowledge of $E(r)$ and σ is sufficient fully to describe these distributions. Empirical evaluation of this assumption becomes crucial. Early work by Mandelbrot (1963) provides evidence that the distribution of price changes in speculative series are not normally distributed but are, in fact, leptokurtic in nature. Subsequent studies report non-normal stock return distributions and non-normal distribution of the residuals from the market model (for example, see Fama, 1965; Affleck-Graves and McDonald, 1989; Richardson and Smith, 1993). Affleck-Graves and McDonald (1989) provide evidence that the normal distribution does not provide a sufficient approximation for monthly returns. Richardson and Smith (1993, p. 301) strongly reject multivariate normality and conclude that 'joint tests suggest much less evidence of normally distributed monthly stock returns than do individual tests'. Given the importance of the normality assumption for finance theory, it is not surprising that much work has been concerned with characterising the nature of the distribution of returns. In general, stock returns are not normally distributed but are leptokurtic with a negative skew. However, what is surprising is that there is little consensus about the cause of such distributions. A potential link between the observed leptokurtism of the probability distributions of stock prices and returns and the decision heuristics adopted by individuals when faced with repeated financial decisions is now offered by way of conjecture.

We begin with the assumption that the trading process is cyclical in nature. An individual trader observes the price distribution of a given share and based on this information alone (note the focus on noise traders as in earlier chapters) makes trade decisions to buy or sell a certain volume of the share. These trade decisions are aggregated by the market and feed back into the determination of the newly observed price distribution. The trading process then begins afresh. If we assume, for a given share, a constant volume of trade across the entire range of the price distribution (depicted in Figure 5.1a), then there is no reason to believe that the resulting price distribution would be anything other than normally distributed

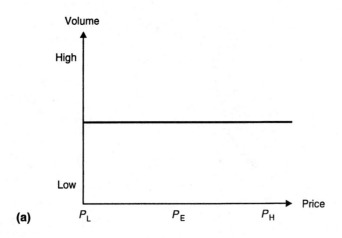

(a)

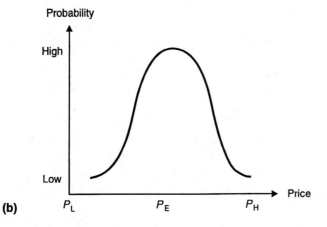

(b)

Figure 5.1 (a) Constant volume of trade across all prices; (b) Normal probability distribution of prices

(depicted in Figure 5.1b). However, is it realistic to assume a constant volume of trade across the range of the price distribution? It is plausible that a more realistic depiction of the volume of trade across the price range is the one contained in Figure 5.2(a). The reason such trading volume may be more realistic is a result of the decision heuristics adopted by individuals in the face of repeated financial decisions. Evidence reported in Chapter 3 indicates that the most successful decision strategies adopted by individuals could be characterised by the 3As of asymmetry, activity and aggression. Indeed, the analysis identified two basic types, a buyer's strategy and a seller's strategy. A buyer's strategy consists of lots of small buy decisions followed by a large sell decision. In contrast, a seller's strategy consists of lots of small sell decisions followed by a large buy decision. It is apparent that whilst all those individuals operating a buyer's strategy will not have identical reservation prices (the

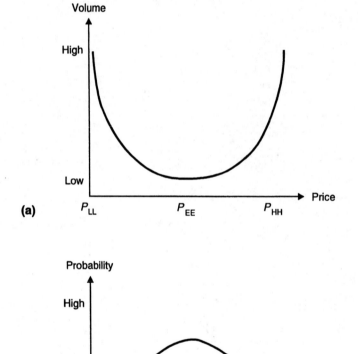

Figure 5.2 (a) High volume of trade at extreme prices; (b) Leptokurtic probability distribution of prices

price at which they will enact their large sell decision), they will have reservation prices that take on similar values. This view is easily justified by the opinion that the higher the price becomes the more obvious it is that the price series has reached, or almost reached, its maximum and the time to sell has arrived. It is possible to suggest then that a large volume of sales will occur over a small range of prices at the high extreme of the price distribution (say, around P_H in Figure 5.1a). Thus, a greater number of traders will be selling a greater volume of shares at this high extreme price range than anywhere else over the price distribution. The reverse argument can be made for those individuals adopting seller's strategies, the result being a greater number of traders buying a greater volume of shares at a low extreme price range (say, around P_L in Figure 5.1a) than anywhere else over the price distribution. The combined result is a high volume of trade at the two extremes of the price range (P_H, P_L) and a relatively lower volume along the mid-range of the price distribution, around which it becomes relatively more difficult to predict the direction of the next change in price.

The volume of trade across the range of prices can no longer be viewed as constant and is more accurately depicted by Figure 5.2(a). The obvious implication is that the decision heuristics adopted by individuals in the face of repeated financial decisions impact on both the size and timing (with reference to prices) of trading decisions. In the cyclical view of the trading process adopted here, these trading decisions ultimately feed into and shape the future price distribution. This cyclical trading process repeats *ad infinitum*. The issue now becomes one of determining the shape of the resultant price distribution. It is proffered here that the impact of the high trade volume at extreme prices is to 'squeeze' the price distribution, effectively truncating the price range and resulting in a leptokurtic distribution (as depicted in Figure 5.2b). Even if we assume that individuals originally face a normally distributed price series, it is possible that this can be transformed into a leptokurtic distribution as a result of decision heuristics adopted in the face of repeated financial decisions. The finance literature is void of any justification for the empirically observed skewed and leptokurtic price/return distributions. Unfortunately, this chapter is unable to prove the above link, owing to design limitations discussed in the following section. However, the argument is intuitively plausible and future experimental work could fruitfully substantiate the link between repeated financial decisions and non-normal distributions.

3. Specifics of the experimental design

In an ideal world, the experimental approach to understanding the distributional properties of repeated financial decision making would mirror the whole micro structure of price setting, jobbing, broking, trading responses, etc. The approach would attempt to capture the influences and responses of a highly dynamic process. Clearly, such an approach is currently beyond the means of experimental scientists. Furthermore, the adoption of a general experimental design for the investigation of a number of interrelated issues, as is the case here, means that compromises in the experimental design are required. The limitations of the experimental design for the purpose of this chapter are discussed below.

First, because of the obvious need for simplicity, the experiment only allows participants to substitute the riskless asset cash for the traded share. As discussed in the previous chapter, one consequence is that the price-elasticity of the demand for the share may be biased downwards because of the lack of close substitutes. The exact impact of this on the distribution of traded responses depends on the constancy of the responses, or otherwise, across the range of prices. This issue is, however, ameliorated to a degree by the absence of transaction costs within the experimental design, a lack of transaction costs being more likely to increase rather than decrease the elasticity of responses to given price changes. Secondly, the riskless asset cash offers a zero rate of return and this may be seen, at first sight, to bias the results. However, given that the research is concerned with how distributions of trading responses correspond to distributions of prices and not with the absolute demand for a share, it is unclear how a zero return to the riskless asset would bias the results. Furthermore, it is difficult to see how the results would be affected by a zero rate of return as compared with the present real rate of return of 2% to 3%. It is for these reasons, and because of its simplicity, that a zero rate of return was chosen for the riskless asset. Thirdly, it could be argued that a final prize of £100 would have the consequence of inducing extreme trading behaviour with a concomitant effect upon the distribution of trading responses (see Chapter 2 for a general discussion of possible tournament effects). In answer to this, such behaviour should have been reduced by the fact that the participants were not fully aware of their relative trading performance. As the experiment was run via open sessions across the whole of five days, it was difficult for the participants to assess relative performance at any one point in time. Furthermore, the selection of the participants from a broad range of faculties should have hampered comparison via personal discussion. Thus, it would have been difficult for individuals to judge the relative benefits of following a risk-seeking strategy.

Whilst the above three limitations offer interesting questions that require further consideration, they do not represent the major limitation of the current experimental design when the intention is to link the empirically observed non-normal price/return distributions with the decision heuristics adopted in the face of repeated financial decisions. The major limitation is a result of the fact that the five price series used were exogenously derived, therefore the size and direction of trades have no impact on the next market price faced. As a result, we can never observe the nature of the resultant price distribution. Unfortunately, this derives from attempting to investigate the wide-ranging issues of concern in the current study. Whilst a common theme runs through the study, distinct issues are investigated. It is clear, therefore, that some form of trade-off is necessary. The use of exogenous price series allows the design to mimic the atomistic price-taking framework at the heart of competitive financial markets and permits a greater degree of control in the investigation of the characteristics of repeated financial decision making undertaken in Chapter 3. Exogenous price series were also required for a controlled analysis of the price-elasticity of demand undertaken in Chapter 4. Thus, a conscious decision was taken not to include endogenous price series in the experimental design and so accept the problems of drawing inferences about the influence of repeated financial decision making on the nature of resultant price/return distributions. The analysis reported below does not provide direct evidence of the relationship, but provides indirect support by investigating four different distribution measures via a comparison of the original price distributions and observed portfolio return distributions.

4. The empirical method

In examining the distributional properties of repeated financial decision making, four different distributions are considered: standardised initial returns (R_t); standardised portfolio returns (PR_t); the shares held (S_t) and the proportion of wealth held in shares $P_tS_t/(P_tS_t + \text{Cash}_t)$, where P_t signifies the price of a share at time t. As a basis of comparison, the initial price series (P_t) faced by the participants are transformed into returns $R_t = (P_t - P_{t-1})/P_{t-1}$. The decision responses of the participants are considered in the form of the returns of their holdings of shares and cash, that is:

$$PR_t = \frac{V_t - V_{t-1}}{V_{t-1}},$$

where $V_t = P_tS_t + \text{Cash}_t$. This measure is chosen because individuals should have, given the incentives on offer, focused their attention on maximising the returns on their portfolio of share and cash. However, the distributions of the shares held (S_t) and the proportion of wealth held as shares $P_tS_t/(P_tS_t + \text{Cash}_t)$, are also used to illustrate the nature of repeated decision making. For ease of comparison, the distributions are standardised via their mean and standard deviation (that is, a standardised return $z_i^* = (R_t - \bar{y})/s$, where returns have mean $= \bar{y}$ and variance $= s^2$ over time t). Comparing the above distributions for the five days of trading, the first four moments of the distributions are computed using:

$$m_1 = \bar{y} = \sum_{i=1}^{n} y_i/n \quad \text{and} \quad m_j = \sum_{i=1}^{n} (y_i - \bar{y})^j/n \quad \text{for} \quad j > 1,$$

where the variance s^2 is m_2; the coefficients of skewness and kurtosis are $m_3/(m_2)^{3/2}$ and $m_4/(m_2)^2$, respectively.

Although the exact distributions of the statistics for sample skewness and kurtosis ratios under the assumption of normality are difficult to obtain (D'Agostino and Pearson, 1973), simulation studies suggest that these sample moment ratio tests are reasonably robust when the direction of the deviation can be ascertained (Pearson et al, 1977). It is for this reason that we illustrate the nature of the distributions via standardised graphs, where need be. As a whole, the summary statistics and standardised graphs provide evidence concerning the distributional properties of repeated financial decision making. Finally, the initial return distributions and the portfolio return distributions are compared by using a Kolmogorov–Smirnov test for normality.[1]

5. Results and analysis

Table 5.1 contains the main body of the results for the five days of decision making, while Figure 5.3 contains graphs of representative distributions. All the days offer similar results and day 4 (Cadbury PLC) has been chosen for illustrative purposes. Rows 1 to 5 of Table 5.1 summarise the nature of the price return series used in the experiment. The sample ratio statistics for skewness and kurtosis indicate that the price return distributions have a marginal positive skew for four of the five days and are platykurtic (that is, the coefficient of kurtosis $k < 3$ and the distribution is less peaked in the centre with shorter tails than is the case for the normal distribution). The five price series were chosen on the basis of selecting 'blue chip' companies and not because of any underlying properties of the price distributions. In other words, no attempt was made to select certain types of price distribution and it is unclear why the chosen companies have the distributions as noted. The data on the portfolio returns are shown in the second section of Table 5.1 (rows 6 to 10). Here, the statistics for skew (row 8) indicate that the process of trading has led to a negative skew in the portfolio returns. Similarly, for each of the days of trading, the kurtosis statistic has increased. Although this only led to a move from platykurtic to leptokurtic distributions on days 4 and 5, it does indicate a general tendency towards non-linear transformation of the underlying series. This is supported by the Kolmogorov–Smirnov statistics of rows 5 and 10, which indicate that the process of trading tended to lead to non-normal distributions (at a 99% level of confidence). In general, the process of repeated decision making led to transformations of a 'leptokurtic' nature.

   Thus, the results imply that one aspect of repeated financial decision making is to take the underlying price series and non-linearly transform it to derive the distribution of the portfolio returns. Before considering this result further, however, it is important to demonstrate that the transformation is a function of repeated financial decision making, rather than an intrinsic result of a mathematical operation. For example, it could be argued that given the means of the share return distributions are all positive, while the cash security has mean zero, the portfolio return, which is a mixture of these two securities, will have, by definition, certain properties. It is not hard to show that if participants are faced with a series of market prices P_i, they can, by their personal choice of balancing (between risky and riskless assets) strategy determine their own portfolio returns, which may or may not reflect the returns that the market makes on the price series. While the market return is $R_m = (P_{i-1} + P_i)/P_i$, the return on a participant's personal portfolio is measured by a change in wealth from period to period. $R_p = (W_{i-1} + W_i)/W_i$, where portfolio value (wealth) for a given period is $W_j = P_j S_j + C_j$ (a combination of risky and riskless assets). If R_m is a probability distribution function, then the choice of an individual's rebalancing strategy may lead to a personal distribution of portfolio returns that could be a linear

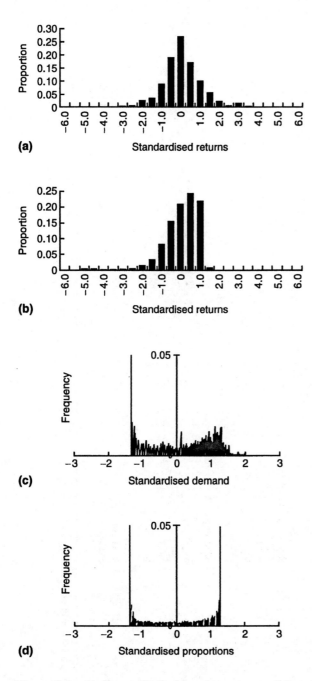

Figure 5.3 Cadbury PLC: (a) price returns; (b) portfolio returns; (c) demand for shares; (d) standard proportion of wealth hel as shares

Table 5.1 Results for five days of decision-making

Row		Days				
		1	2	3	4	5
R_t						
1	Mean	0.034	0.015	0.010	0.069	0.200
2	Variance	1.026	0.706	0.767	1.006	0.801
3	Skew	−0.051	0.260	0.261	0.330	0.004
4	Kurtosis	0.940	0.451	0.515	0.902	0.662
5	Kolmogorov–Smirnov	1.348	1.342	1.460	1.521	1.468
PR_t						
6	Mean	0.015	−0.010	0.040	−0.010	−0.313
7	Variance	0.956	1.014	0.843	1.096	0.651
8	Skew	−1.146	−0.683	−1.487	−2.123	−1.612
9	Kurtosis	1.540	0.460	2.705	7.178	3.232
10	Kolmogorov–Smirnov	1.739*	1.636*	2.226*	1.838*	2.355*
S_t						
11	Mean	48.1332	85.9906	51.0303	60.7612	58.6470
12	Variance	1822.5482	4911.3243	1717.5799	2045.7207	1835.2138
13	Skew	0.5296	0.3916	0.3706	0.0199	0.0776
14	Kurtosis	1.9521	1.8672	2.2393	1.6014	1.8244
P_tS_t						
15	Mean	0.3804	0.4590	0.4712	0.5202	0.5406
16	Variance	0.1098	0.1260	0.1358	0.1402	0.1393
$(P_tS_t + Cash_t)$						
17	Skew	0.4641	0.1714	0.1116	−0.1189	−0.1953
18	Kurtosis	1.8211	1.5662	1.4874	1.4457	1.4682

*Significant at a 99% level of confidence.

transformation of R_m, or a non-linear transformation of R_m or entirely independent of the R_m distribution. Consider, for example, three decision strategies:

Strategy 1 Participants maintain a fixed proportion of wealth in the risk asset throughout with

$$P_j S_j = \alpha W_i \quad \text{and} \quad C_j = (1 - \alpha) W_i, \quad 0 \leqslant \alpha \leqslant 1.$$

In this scenario, for period 0, the following can be written:

$$W_0 = P_0 S_0 + C_0 \tag{3}$$

with

$$C_0 = (1 - \alpha) W_0 \tag{4}$$

and

$$P_0 S_0 = \alpha W_0. \tag{5}$$

In the next period, the price changes so that $W_1 = P_1 S_0 + C_0$ before the portfolio is rebalanced.

Using (3), (4) and (5) the value of the risky asset in period 1 can be written as:

$$P_1 S_0 = W_1 - (1 - \alpha) W_0. \tag{6}$$

From (5) and (6), the relationship between market price returns and the portfolio returns can be constructed as follows:

$$\frac{P_1 S_0 - P_0 S_0}{P_0 S_0} = \frac{W_1 - W_0 + \alpha W_0 - \alpha W_0}{\alpha W_0} \tag{7}$$

With a little reduction, the following applies:

$$\frac{P_1 - P_0}{P_0} = \frac{W_1 - W_0}{\alpha W_0}, \quad \text{i.e.} \quad \alpha R_m = R_p. \tag{8}$$

Now if $R_m \sim N(\mu, \sigma^2)$, then participants who adopt the strategy just described will merely affect a linear transformation on the market returns to generate their own portfolio returns, so portfolio returns will also be normally distributed with a static shift to the left $R_p \sim N(\alpha\mu, \sigma^2)$. The basic characteristics of the distribution are preserved. On aggregation, participants' decisions will generate a distribution of market returns shifted to the left or right (as a point of interest, this may be a way of viewing what might be happening during times of increasing or decreasing confidence in the market place).

Strategy 2   This considers the extreme cases of strategy 1. Suppose participants keep all their wealth entirely in the risky asset $\alpha = 1$. Then:

$$\frac{P_1 - P_0}{P_0} = \frac{W_1 - W_0}{W_0}$$

portfolio returns are the same as market returns for each participant and the market aggregate distribution is completely unaltered.

Strategy 3   This set $\alpha = 0$, i.e. only cash is held, in which case the participants wealth from period to period is independent of market price movements and portfolio returns are zero.

It is possible to go on postulating balancing strategies but just in these simple cases it has been shown that the strategy is crucial to the shape of the distribution of portfolio returns. Introducing skew and/or kurtosis can be achieved by defining a transformation in which the strategy is to hold shares logarithmically, geometrically or inversely proportional to the price. While such possibilities are interesting, they are not a direct concern of the present study, which is an empirical study of behaviour in an experimental setting. None the less, given that almost any kind of transformation is possible, what is observed, on aggregate, is that participants in the current experiment skewed the distribution of market returns in generating their own portfolio returns, thus suggesting that when deriving portfolio returns the strategic behaviour of re-balancing strategies leads to non-linear transformations of market returns.

Having determined that the non-linear transformation of the underlying price return distributions that generate the observed portfolio returns reflect repeated financial decision making rather than a mathematical operation, a result of particular interest in the present context is the negative skew introduced into the distribution of portfolio returns. Although it is impossible to draw definitive explanations of this result, there are explanations that may be followed from prior work (see Krugman, 1989; Dixit, 1989; Ansic, 1995). It may be the case that on the gains side of the returns distribution, participants do not take full advantage of the potential returns because of risk aversion. For example, if a decision maker had perfect foresight and was able to assess correctly that prices would rise, he/she would rationally commit 100% of his/her available cash resources into shares in order to maximise the potential returns available from the expected future price rise. However, without perfect foresight, risk-averse decision makers might invest only a proportion of their available cash resources into the shares when a price rise was expected. The result of this form of behaviour is that portfolios increase in value when expectations prove correct but not to the extent that might have been possible if all available cash had been committed. In this situation, the distribution of portfolio returns will have less weight in the tail on the gains side than the original returns.

On the loss side of the distribution of returns something different may be occurring—a case of trade hysteresis. In this situation, a decision maker with perfect foresight will immediately withdraw all his wealth from the risky asset as soon as he knows that the price of the asset is in decline; to stay in the declining market would mean certain losses. However, if individuals do not have perfect foresight, the trade hysteresis hypothesis predicts that a decision maker will adopt a 'wait-and-see' policy before liquidating his/her shares in the hope that prices may soon turn upward and losses will be recouped. Hence, once a decision maker has made a commitment to hold some shares, he/she will not lightly discard those shares, and so when prices are in decline losses are exacerbated by a tendency towards 'stickiness' in response, the result of this form of behaviour being that more weight appears on the loss side of the portfolio returns distribution than appeared in the original returns distribution. The net impact of less weight placed on the gains side tail and more weight on the loss side tail of portfolio returns gives rise to the negatively skewed distributions observed in the current results. If the above explanations are pertinent, then the buying and selling of shares is a non symmetrical decision process.

Before drawing any conclusions, further understanding of the decision making process is needed. This can be gained from considering the shares held per decision and the proportion of wealth held as shares per decision. Although statistics are provided for each of these in sections 3 and 4 of Table 5.1, respectively, graphs are more illuminating in this particular instance. The graph of the shares held per decision (Figure 5.3c) illustrates two peaks at the extremes of the distribution. The peak at the lower end of the distribution corresponds to the lower bound of holding zero shares. The upper part of the distribution is not bounded, hence the more dispersed nature of the peak. The two peaks at the extremes of the distribution indicate that the participants' behaviour tended towards a strategy of moving heavily into and out of the share in question at the extremes. This initial hypothesis is supported by consideration of the graphs of the distributions of the proportion of wealth held as shares. Figure 5.3(d) shows two pronounced peaks at the extremes of the distribution—the participants held either a zero proportion of their wealth as shares or they held all their wealth in the form of shares. This form of behaviour is consistent with the process described above for the change in skew of the distribution, in that the present twin peaks correspond to the situation where it is obvious that the shares should be sold or bought. In other words, at the extremes of the price distribution (low or high), the choice to be made (buy or sell) becomes increasingly clear. None the less, even if the current explanations turn out to be false, in the light of the twin peaks of repeated decision making and the noted change in skew, it is difficult not to conclude that the repeated decision responses to price returns data are non linear in nature.

4. Discussion and conclusions

In exploring the distributional properties of repeated financial decision making, this study has found evidence of individuals making decisions such that initial price return distributions when generating portfolio returns are non-linearly transformed via a negative skew and a tendency towards 'leptokurtism'. Essentially, the emphasis on asymmetric (buying and selling) trading strategies will become more pronounced at the extremes of the price distributions. In other words, traders feel more secure in shifting greater volumes of shares at the extreme prices. This twin-peaked distribution of trading volume results in fatter tails for the price/return distributions; that is, leptokurtic distributions. If it is accepted that repeated financial decision making may well be the cause of leptokurtic price/return distributions, then future experimental work could fruitfully evaluate this conjecture.

6 Conclusions

This study has focused on the repeated nature of financial trading decisions. Although the financial markets are characterised by repeated decision making, there has been almost a total absence of analysis into this aspect of their operation. Essentially, mainstream finance theory makes no distinction between one-off decisions that populate so much of decision theory and the repeated decisions that characterise the financial stock markets. In making a start on this research, this monograph has described the results of a large-scale experimental study.

Chapter 1 offered a backcloth to the later chapters by comparing and contrasting the assumptions of the mainstream finance model with the characteristics of the situations likely to be faced by practical investors. Essentially, the chapter offered evidence of the need to offer a richer description of the way individuals potentially trade with stocks. For example, the mainstream model's emphasis on investors seeking to maximise end-state (terminal) wealth was contrasted to the possibility that they may be concerned to compare wealth with some predetermined benchmark. In this light, the gains and losses of wealth are likely to be as important as the absolute level of wealth. Equally, the chapter questioned the validity of the subjective expected utility (SEU) model, which lies at the heart of mainstream finance, as a means of describing the way in which individuals cope with the stresses and strains of repeated trading. It was argued that the SEU model is too demanding in its information requirements and decision calculus to offer a meaningful description of repeated trading behaviour, hence the need for an experimental study to begin to uncover the types of heuristics investors might use to deal with situations of repeated trading.

The second chapter gave a general introduction to the design of the experiment. This general discussion of the experimental method and its associated strengths was followed by a detailed exposition of the adopted design. The experiment consisted of 62 participants individually buying and selling a stock during a trading period of 40 minutes on each of five consecutive days (real time). During each trading period the participants sat at a trading screen for 40 minutes and with the aid of written instructions they had to buy/sell the identified blue-chip stock. The trading screen facing each participant consisted of a past history of the daily closing prices of the stock, an opening inventory of stocks, the current stock price and a trading box in which they could buy/sell or view the past prices of the stock. The price series faced by the participants consisted of real quoted closing price data for a given share each day. A different blue-chip UK share was chosen for each of the five trading days.

The experiment was designed to capture the nature of the repeated financial decision making of active investors within a trading environment. Participants were motivated fully to disclose their responses to the changing prices of a share. An analysis of these responses has allowed direct conclusions to be drawn concerning the nature of the trading behaviour of individuals and the consequences of such for the nature of the demand curve for shares and the distribution properties of securities. By providing price series that differed in terms of their levels, ranges and degrees of volatility, the experiment was designed to ensure robust results. Although the final part of Chapter 2 was concerned with highlighting weaknesses of the experimental design, it concluded that the design did not suffer from fundamental problems.

The focus of Chapter 3 was the reporting of the experimental results in terms of the specific nature of repeated trading decisions in a financial context and the characteristics of successful trading decision strategies. From an analysis of the data, three conclusions were drawn. First, even in the face of non-stationary price series, individuals adopt stationary (consistent) decision series. That is, when confronted with shifting distributions of prices, individuals adopt reasonably firm decision strategies. Secondly, these strategies are such that decisions across time are related, with current decisions being most influenced by the more recent decisions. Hence, in a repeated decision context, individual decisions are not seen as isolated one-off events but rather are dealt with as being part of a series of such decisions. Given the costs of dealing with such a decision context, it is perhaps not surprising that individuals seem to adopt decision strategies that minimise on information and 'decision' costs. Thirdly, the exploratory analysis also considered, via the use of runs tests, whether the decision series of the individuals displayed consistently recognisable, systematic patterns of behaviour. Two basic trading patterns emerged: a seller's strategy where an individual bought a large inventory of a share at a given price and then sold small parcels of the share from the inventory, and a buyer's strategy where the individual primarily held wealth as cash and then slowly bought small parcels of the share. The successful trading emanating from these two asymmetric strategies had two salient characteristics—activity and aggression. The successful traders used the simplicity of focus of the strategies to make a lot more decisions and trade more volume. Thus, successful active trading within a repeated decision context has three features—asymmetry, activity and aggression, the 3As of successful trading.

Given the above results and conclusions, two issues to be considered were how such decision behaviour might affect the modelling of decisions and the operation of markets. In terms of modelling decisions, the results clearly indicated that within the context of repeated decisions under uncertainty, individuals seem to adopt decision strategies that economise on the obvious decision and information costs via heuristics that make use of past decisions and that focus on one aspect (buy or sell) of transactions. In addition, the costs of repeated decision making seem to be reduced by the continued use of a particular decision strategy. In essence, individuals in the current context minimise on decision costs by focusing on one side of the decision; that is, they adopt either buy or sell strategies. The results suggest, therefore, that repeated decisions may not be treated as isolated one-off events that can be handled with a purely forward-looking mentality but, rather, decision makers cope with the high decision and information costs of repeated decision making under uncertainty via strategies that make use of past decisions. In terms of the impact of the current results on the behaviour of markets, at the most obvious level the stationary responses of individuals to non-stationary price series should have the beneficial effect of lending stability to markets. However, given the use of past decisions within the noted decision processes, the obvious benefits of stability might be replaced by the less attractive characteristic of market 'stickiness'; that is, where there is a slow response to changes in market parameters. Whether the noted decision processes lead to stability or stickiness, and this will ultimately depend on the exact characteristics of the particular market of interest, it is possible that the success associated with asymmetric decision strategies (focusing either on the sell or the buy side of market transactions) might be one explanation of the cyclical nature of many markets. In general, therefore, further research could usefully explore how the characteristics of repeated decision making discussed here might be used to explain the commonly noted market features of hysteresis and cycles.

The fourth chapter considered how the decision processes and choice of trading strategy adopted by individuals, in aggregate, might impact upon the demand function of the traded security. The issue is clearly important since a number of theorems of finance, as well as the calculation of take-over premiums, depend upon the demand curves for stocks being horizontal or highly price-elastic. For example, the active arbitrage mechanism that underpins the efficiency results of the finance literature depends upon a demand curve that is horizontal or displays a high degree of price-elasticity. Thus, much of finance theory is based on the premise that the demand curve for stocks is highly price-elastic (or horizontal in the extreme) and, therefore, the determination of the type of demand function emanating from the noted trading behaviours is important.

Chapter 4 concluded that the noted trading behaviour gave rise to highly elastic demand curves. Thus, although the decision-making framework that individuals seem to adopt in the context of repeated financial decisions (that is, based on past prices and asymmetric in outlook) is somewhat different from that proposed in finance theory, one of the key outcomes of such behaviour—an elastic demand curve for stocks—is identical to that assumed by finance theory. This suggests, to us at least, that finance theory might usefully explore the implications of richer decision models. It is not apparent that the whole edifice of finance theory need crumble and, indeed, further insights might be gained by considering how different decision models (for example, asymmetric buy and sell trading strategies) might come together to create financial markets. In fact, some of the more obvious phenomena of financial markets—at times volatile, cyclical and sticky—might begin to be understood if we move away from viewing market participants as always responding with a symmetric and purely future-looking perspective.

The common feature linking the previous chapters is their focus on repeated financial decision making and, more specifically, the identification of the nature and defining characteristics of repeated decisions. Chapter 5 continued this theme by discussing the possible implications of the noted trading behaviours for observed portfolio returns and price/return distributions. The discussion started from the basis that earlier analysis identified two basic types of trading behaviour: buying and selling strategies—a buyer's strategy consisting of lots of small buy decisions followed by a large sell decision and a seller's strategy consisting of lots of small sell decisions followed by a large buy decision. Furthermore, it argued that whilst all those individuals operating a buyer's strategy will not have identical reservation prices (the price at which they will enact their large sell decision), they will have reservation prices that take on similar values. This view was easily justified by the opinion that the higher the price becomes the more obvious it is that the price series has reached, or almost reached, its maximum and the time to sell has arrived. It was then suggested that a large volume of sales will occur over a small range of prices at the high extreme of the price distribution; that is, a greater number of traders will be selling a greater volume of shares at the extremes of the price range than anywhere else. The reverse argument was made for those individuals adopting seller's strategies. The combined result would be a high volume of trade at the two extremes of the price range and a relatively lower volume along the mid-range of the price distribution, around which it becomes relatively more difficult to predict the direction of the next change in price.

Therefore, the volume of trade across the range of prices can no longer be viewed as constant and the obvious implication is that the decision heuristics adopted by individuals in the face of repeated financial decisions impact on both the size and timing (with reference to prices) of trading decisions. In the cyclical view of the trading process adopted in the chapter, these trading decisions ultimately feed into and shape the future price distribution. This cyclical trading process repeats *ad infinitum*. The issue now becomes one of determining the shape of the resultant price distribution. It was suggested that the impact of the high trade volume at extreme prices is to 'squeeze' the price distribution, effectively truncating the price range and resulting in a leptokurtic distribution. Essentially, the discussion suggested that even if individuals originally face a normally distributed price series, it is possible that this can be transformed into a leptokurtic distribution as a result of decision heuristics adopted in the face of repeated financial decisions. In summary, in exploring the distributional properties of repeated financial decision making, Chapter 5 found evidence of individuals making decisions such that initial price return distributions when generating portfolio returns are non linearly transformed via a negative skew and a tendency towards 'leptokurtism'. Essentially, the emphasis on asymmetric (buying and selling) trading strategies tends to become more pronounced at the extremes of the price distributions through traders feeling more secure in shifting greater volumes of shares at extreme prices. This twin-peaked distribution of trading volume results in fatter tails for the price/return distributions; that is, leptokurtic distributions. If it is accepted that repeated financial decision making may well be the cause of leptokurtic price/return distributions, future experimental work could fruitfully explore this conclusion.

In conclusion, this monograph has reported the results of a large-scale experimental study into the types of behaviour individuals display when trading with stocks. The results indicate that individuals focus on one side of the buy/sell decision; that is, individuals show a fundamental asymmetry in the way they approach the stock market. Also, success is found to be a function of being active in the market and not being afraid to be aggressive—if the market moves, then react and react with passion. Furthermore, these trading behaviours of individuals lead to elastic demand curves for stocks (an important condition for market efficiency) and they offer an explanation for the leptokurtic nature of stock returns (a noted anomaly of stock markets). In other words, the noted trading behaviours are consistent both with one aspect of market efficiency and an important empirical feature of stock markets. Given the above, it is hoped that the current results are sufficiently interesting for others to want to follow the research lead offered here. If this is achieved, then we may gain greater insights into markets that are increasingly important for ever larger sections of society. Such an achievement would allow us to develop theories and understanding that move on from the simplistic notions of market efficiency and stories of 'gambling casinos'!

Appendices

Appendix I: The shares experiment instructions

General

This experiment will involve you in a stock market trading situation, in which you have £150 with which to buy a particularly well-known share. You will also be given an endowment of 75 shares at the beginning to sell or keep as you wish. As time goes on, you will be able to buy or sell shares with your money and stocks of shares, and after each trade the price (value) of the shares will change. The changing prices that you will be exposed to are the *actual* market fluctuations in share price movements for the particular share that occurred in the stockmarket over a certain period of time. Your job is to increase your total wealth by trading. You will be paid at the rate of 3p for every £1 you can earn above the starting endowment you were given.

The experiment will last for five days, and you will need to come every day at your convenience between 9.30 a.m. and 5.00 p.m. to work for approximately 40 min on the computer terminal. Each day you will be trading on a different stock, and you will start each day with £150 and 75 shares.

To get paid at the end of this experiment you must complete all five days' work.

As an incentive to try extra hard, we are offering a £100 prize to the best overall trader.

Appendix II

Table 1 Autocorrelation coefficients: Day 1

ID	n	Lag k 1	2	3	4	5	10	15	20	25	Dickey–Fuller z_t		D_t		Class
2	51	0.43	0.14	0.29	0.4	0.64	0.31	0.11	−0.2	0.09	5.15	S	9.70	S	AR
4	477	0.96	0.91	0.87	0.83	0.79	0.68	0.59	0.49	0.44	3.68	S	22.46	S	AR
5	115	0.86	0.71	0.6	0.62	0.5	0.29	0.11	0.32	0.16	4.54	S	12.15	S	AR
6	309	0.96	0.9	0.84	0.8	0.76	0.56	0.49	0.39	0.23	3.50	S	17.21	S	AR
8	437	0.9	0.8	0.73	0.71	0.69	0.54	0.6	0.42	0.46	5.89	S	22.44	S	AR
9	105	0.84	0.64	0.57	0.45	0.25	0.09	0.28	−0.4	−0.5	4.01	S	11.05	S	AR
11	125	0.63	0.42	0.3	0.29	0.33	0.2	0.05	−0.1	−0.1	6.17	S	13.89	S	AR
13	137	0.81	0.63	0.47	0.27	0.06	−0.2	0.21	0.1	0.01	4.37	S	11.98	S	AR
14	115	0.91	0.83	0.75	0.68	0.64	0.46	0.13	−0.1	−0.2	2.79		11.54	S	I
17	59	0.27	0.32	0.13	0.21	0.1	0.04	0.16	−0.1	−0.3	5.71	S	13.25	S	ARMA
18	65	0.12	−0.1	−0.1	−0.2	−0.1	0.05	0.03	−0.1	−0.3	7.01	S	12.26	S	ARMA
19	442	0.95	0.9	0.86	0.81	0.76	0.46	0.19	0.11	0.16	3.59	S	20.80	S	AR
20	450	0.98	0.96	0.94	0.92	0.89	0.75	0.58	0.44	0.29	2.92	S	21.61	S	AR
23	144	0.85	0.76	0.73	0.62	0.52	0.28	0	−0.2	−0.3	3.86	S	14.68	S	AR
24	164	0.85	0.71	0.56	0.41	0.31	−0.2	−0.2	−0.3	−0.1	4.14	S	13.27	S	AR
26	348	0.76	0.55	0.44	0.43	0.39	0.3	0.35	0.32	0.24	8.01	S	21.13	S	AR
27	276	0.95	0.91	0.86	0.81	0.76	0.53	0.43	0.37	0.18	3.62	S	17.51	S	AR
28	66	0.9	0.81	0.58	0.34	0.12	−0.5	−0.2	−0.1	0.37	2.50		8.77	S	I
29	111	0.9	0.81	0.74	0.68	0.63	0.4	0.09	0.09	0.01	3.23	S	11.32	S	AR
30	271	0.69	0.75	0.62	0.52	0.41	0.1	0.07	0.25	−0.1	5.04	S	16.97	S	AR
32	110	0.89	0.4	0.11	0	−0.2	0	−0.1	0.19	−0.2	5.12	S	11.60	S	ARMA
34	106	0.96	0.92	0.86	0.84	0.79	0.59	0.23	0.12	0.22	2.09		11.52	S	I
35	58	0.63	0.15	0.1	0.43	0.49	−0.2	−0.5	−0.1	−0.1	4.31	S	8.41	S	AR
37	243	0.94	0.89	0.83	0.78	0.73	0.46	0.21	−0.1	−0.3	3.22	S	16.12	S	AR
38	77	0.72	0.43	0.16	0.01	0.13	0.13	−0.1	−0.3	−0.1	4.36	S	9.50	S	ARMA
39	167	0.89	0.75	0.6	0.44	0.3	0.1	0.03	0.12	−0.3	3.84	S	12.13	S	AR
40	283	0.95	0.88	0.84	0.77	0.7	0.48	0.45	0.24	0.1	3.89	S	16.45	S	AR
41	188	0.75	0.67	0.61	0.51	0.4	0.26	0.12	−0.2	−0.5	6.00	S	18.68	S	AR
42	151	0.9	0.76	0.65	0.62	0.49	0.29	0.34	0.26	0.32	4.60	S	13.03	S	AR
43	161	0.95	0.89	0.84	0.78	0.7	0.33	0.01	−0.2	−0.4	2.63		13.05	S	I
44	102	0.87	0.71	0.49	0.44	0.43	0.43	0.12	0.16	−0.2	4.90	S	13.51	S	AR
46	88	0.88	0.78	0.69	0.55	0.34	−0.3	−0.2	0.24	−0.1	3.83	S	10.11	S	AR
47	51	0.43	0.22	0.32	0.39	0.51	0.28	0	−0.1	−0.4	4.91	S	10.19	S	AR
49	180	0.91	0.8	0.66	0.55	0.46	0	0	−0.2	−0.5	3.87	S	13.01	S	AR
50	159	0.89	0.81	0.73	0.59	0.42	−0.1	−0.1	0.22	0.25	3.70	S	13.75	S	AR
52	234	0.98	0.95	0.92	0.89	0.85	0.69	0.45	0.05	−0.2	3.06	S	15.43	S	AR
53	191	0.86	0.74	0.62	0.5	0.41	0.36	0.17	0.11	0	4.89	S	15.11	S	AR
54	88	0.87	0.74	0.6	0.39	0.11	−0.5	0	−0.4	−0.6	4.62	S	8.69	S	ARMA
57	91	0.79	0.57	0.38	0.16	0.03	−0.2	−0.1	−0.2	0.03	4.30	S	10.91	S	ARMA
58	50	0.82	0.44	0.1	0.11	0.09	0	−0.3	−0.1	0	3.33	S	6.62	S	ARMA
60	145	1	0.98	0.97	0.95	0.94	0.83	0.66	0.51	0.3	1.54		9.30	S	I
61	64	0.73	0.53	0.41	0.44	0.5	0.05	−0.3	0	−0.2	4.02	S	11.68	S	AR

Table 2 Autocorrelation coefficients: Day 2

ID	n	1	2	3	4	5	10	15	20	25	z_t		D_t		Class
						Lag k					Dickey–Fuller				
1	64	0.28	−0.1	0	0	0.17	0.19	−0.3	0	0.23	6.36	S	10.53	S	ARMA
2	425	0.94	0.88	0.82	0.75	0.69	0.44	0.28	0.09	0.01	4.11	S	19.32	S	AR
4	343	0.99	0.99	0.97	0.95	0.83	0.82	0.71	0.6	0.54	2.44		17.24	S	I
5	136	0.86	0.77	0.73	0.64	0.57	0.44	0.37	0.29	0.51	4.93	S	15.23	S	AR
6	442	0.87	0.79	0.72	0.65	0.59	0.33	0.18	0.17	0.15	6.55	S	25.27	S	AR
7	137	0.98	0.96	0.92	0.86	0.78	0.48	0.42	0.46	0.16	1.94		13.98	S	I
8	462	0.95	0.91	0.86	0.81	0.75	0.53	0.28	0.1	0	3.92	S	22.68	S	AR
9	83	0.87	0.75	0.61	0.46	0.35	−0.3	−0.3	0.09	−0.3	3.22	S	10.97	S	AR
11	71	0.94	0.82	0.74	0.65	0.45	−0.3	−0.4	0.03	0	2.37		8.59	S	I
12	65	0.39	0.05	−0.2	−0.1	0.16	0	0.1	0.25	0	6.01	S	9.05	S	ARMA
14	98	0.74	0.38	0.04	−0.2	−0.3	−0.1	0.04	0.29	−0.3	4.51	S	10.14	S	AR
15	68	0.57	0.63	0.48	0.1	0.54	−0.3	0.22	0.47	0.37	6.55	S	17.41	S	ARMA
17	66	−0.5	0.25	0.14	−0.1	0.29	0.32	0.06	−0.2	0.06	12.3	S	20.22	S	MA
19	198	1	0.99	0.99	0.98	0.97	0.95	0.94	0.88	0.82	1.75		14.97	S	I
20	419	1	1	0.99	0.99	0.99	0.97	0.95	0.9	0.84	2.34		20.73	S	I
21	164	0.74	0.53	0.42	0.33	0.25	0.02	0	−0.2	−0.1	6.16	S	15.75	S	AR
23	188	0.82	0.68	0.56	0.48	0.35	0.3	−0.1	−0.3	−0.3	5.02	S	16.06	S	AR
24	273	0.81	0.64	0.48	0.34	0.17	−0.2	−0.2	−0.1	0	6.36	S	18.27	S	ARMA
26	325	0.84	0.68	0.61	0.5	0.44	0.01	−0.1	−0.1	−0.2	5.96	S	20.40	S	AR
27	523	0.99	0.97	0.96	0.94	0.93	0.82	0.73	0.69	0.66	2.53		21.10	S	I
30	696	0.93	0.86	0.78	0.69	0.6	0.36	0.26	0.2	0.15	6.45	S	27.70	S	AR
32	172	0.76	0.56	0.34	0.2	0	0.08	0.06	0.08	−0.1	6.30	S	15.12	S	ARMA
34	429	0.99	0.99	0.99	0.99	0.98	0.95	0.91	0.84	0.79	1.03		17.73	S	I
35	56	0.88	0.91	0.89	0.88	0.83	0.64	0.31	0.05	−0.6	2.24		9.44	S	I
36	64	0.48	0.25	0.15	0.26	0.4	0	−0.1	−0.1	0	4.85	S	10.64	S	ARMA
37	69	0.96	0.91	0.88	0.82	0.7	0.29	−0.2	−0.7	−0.9	2.61		8.04	S	I
38	50	0.72	0.53	0.37	0.16	0	−0.1	0.06	−0.3	−0.5	3.26	S	7.96	S	ARMA
39	389	0.96	0.94	0.91	0.89	0.86	0.7	0.5	0.39	0.4	3.09	S	20.92	S	AR
40	398	0.99	0.98	0.97	0.96	0.95	0.88	0.79	0.68	0.59	2.39		22.75	S	I
41	551	0.89	0.79	0.73	0.67	0.62	0.55	0.4	0.29	0.35	7.15	S	25.41	S	AR
42	187	0.93	0.87	0.8	0.74	0.61	0.24	−0.1	−0.3	−0.3	4.52	S	14.26	S	AR
43	448	0.98	0.96	0.95	0.94	0.93	0.89	0.87	0.86	0.85	2.61		27.68	S	I
47	134	0.5	0.3	0.16	0	−0.1	−0.1	−0.2	0.13	−0.1	7.24	S	16.41	S	ARMA
49	205	0.94	0.84	0.82	0.77	0.7	0.34	0.14	0.2	0.44	3.79	S	13.84	S	AR
50	144	0.94	0.84	0.74	0.65	0.55	0.1	−0.2	−0.2	−0.1	2.84		10.81	S	I
52	151	0.99	0.98	0.96	0.93	0.89	0.66	0.4	0.04	−0.3	1.80		11.05	S	I
53	225	0.99	0.99	0.98	0.98	0.96	0.77	0.42	0.08	−0.2	2.52		15.21	S	I
54	201	0.97	0.95	0.92	0.9	0.88	0.8	0.74	0.66	0.57	2.73		15.05	S	I
57	170	0.93	0.83	0.72	0.62	0.52	0	−0.3	−0.3	−0.1	3.09	S	12.03	S	AR
58	217	1	0.99	0.98	0.96	0.93	0.75	0.62	0.52	0.34	1.45		12.03	S	I

Table 3　Autocorrelation coefficients: Day 3

ID	n	Lag k									Dickey–Fuller				Class
		1	2	3	4	5	10	15	20	25	z_t		D_t		
1	116	0.29	−0.1	−0.1	−0.1	−0.1	0.09	−0.2	−0.2	0.48	13.3	S	14.09	S	ARMA
4	82	0.94	0.81	0.65	0.52	0.38	−0.2	−0.9	−0.6	0	2.73		8.66	S	I
5	175	0.9	0.81	0.73	0.66	0.59	0.29	0.06	−0.3	−0.3	3.79	S	14.40	S	AR
6	450	0.73	0.65	0.56	0.52	0.51	0.29	0.22	0.16	0.04	9.61	S	29.13	S	AR
7	88	1	0.98	0.95	0.92	0.88	0.66	0.45	0.34	0.02	0.65		8.13	S	I
8	393	0.97	0.95	0.92	0.9	0.88	0.75	0.64	0.57	0.51	2.97	S	19.77	S	AR
11	112	0.9	0.75	0.58	0.4	0.22	−0.5	−0.3	0.13	−0.1	3.30	S	10.46	S	AR
12	77	0.32	0.23	0.37	0.14	0.05	−0.3	−0.2	0	0.16	6.50	S	13.51	S	ARMA
15	92	0.48	0.25	−0.2	0.03	−0.4	−0.3	−0.2	0.05	−0.5	6.71	S	14.47	S	AR
16	143	−0.3	0.02	0.1	−0.2	0.06	0	0.09	−0.1	0.03	14.2	S	22.11	S	MA
17	175	0.82	0.67	0.4	−0.3	0.07	−0.2	−0.2	−0.2	−0.1	8.78	S	19.28	S	ARMA
18	495	0.95	0.87	0.8	0.71	0.61	0.28	0.03	−0.2	−0.3	5.75	S	21.21	S	AR
19	323	0.95	0.91	0.86	0.83	0.79	0.65	0.54	0.44	0.35	5.36	S	18.56	S	AR
20	367	0.95	0.87	0.78	0.71	0.66	0.51	0.44	0.45	0.25	4.91	S	18.25	S	AR
21	298	0.95	0.89	0.84	0.76	0.68	0.26	0.08	−0.2	−0.4	4.02	S	17.14	S	AR
23	273	0.98	0.96	0.93	0.89	0.84	0.55	0.27	0.08	0	2.43		14.93	S	I
24	281	0.9	0.8	0.68	0.56	0.44	0	−0.3	−0.3	−0.1	4.28	S	15.75	S	AR
25	90	0.88	0.72	0.57	0.41	0.26	−0.3	−0.4	−0.2	0.05	2.74		9.11	S	I
26	403	0.74	0.56	0.36	0.23	0.15	0.1	0.23	0.39	0.17	10.1	S	26.23	S	ARMA
27	512	0.96	0.93	0.89	0.85	0.81	0.62	0.42	0.23	0.13	3.95	S	23.04	S	AR
28	53	0.3	0.17	0.08	0.2	0.16	−0.3	−0.3	−0.2	0.06	5.66	S	11.24	S	ARMA
29	341	0.84	0.68	0.59	0.54	0.5	0.31	0.25	0.11	0.01	6.13	S	19.55	S	AR
30	784	0.94	0.88	0.82	0.79	0.76	0.58	0.39	0.28	0.2	6.90	S	29.04	S	AR
31	53	0.47	0.24	0	0	0	−0.1	−0.1	−0.4	0.01	4.37	S	9.17	S	ARMA
32	242	0.51	0.15	0	0	0.03	0.05	0.05	−0.1	−0.1	9.44	S	18.82	S	ARMA
34	480	0.98	0.97	0.95	0.94	0.92	0.84	0.73	0.64	0.49	2.82		22.34	S	I
37	180	0.89	0.79	0.66	0.51	0.36	−0.1	−0.2	0	0.02	3.70	S	13.42	S	AR
38	76	0.49	0.25	0.29	0	0	0.08	−0.1	−0.2	0.16	5.40	S	11.65	S	ARMA
39	243	0.93	0.84	0.76	0.68	0.6	0.22	−0.1	−0.2	−0.2	3.52	S	14.73	S	AR
40	306	0.95	0.88	0.82	0.75	0.68	0.44	0.37	0.43	0.32	3.58	S	16.29	S	AR
41	381	0.94	0.92	0.87	0.83	0.77	0.57	0.4	0.25	0.14	4.64	S	24.37	S	AR
42	184	0.85	0.73	0.65	0.57	0.53	0.23	0.03	−0.2	−0.2	4.62	S	15.89	S	AR
43	465	0.9	0.84	0.79	0.73	0.68	0.45	0.31	0.17	0.11	4.95	S	26.65	S	AR
44	84	0.65	0.33	0.06	−0.2	−0.2	0.08	−0.3	−0.2	−0.1	5.11	S	11.15	S	ARMA
45	111	0.93	0.91	0.91	0.86	0.85	0.7	0.64	0.36	0.27	4.63	S	19.03	S	ARMA
47	133	0.42	−0.1	0.06	0.16	0.02	−0.2	0	0.07	0	7.94	S	13.37	S	ARMA
49	335	0.93	0.88	0.85	0.8	0.74	0.37	−0.1	−0.3	−0.4	3.97	S	18.57	S	AR
50	270	0.96	0.92	0.84	0.77	0.7	0.26	0	−0.2	−0.2	3.73	S	18.19	S	AR
52	263	0.92	0.84	0.77	0.71	0.64	0.25	−0.2	−0.3	−0.5	3.86	S	16.26	S	AR
53	226	0.89	0.8	0.7	0.61	0.54	0.14	−0.2	−0.4	−0.4	4.56	S	16.88	S	AR
54	120	0.87	0.76	0.66	0.57	0.48	0	−0.4	−0.5	−0.3	3.19	S	11.36	S	AR
56	76	−0.3	0	0	−0.1	−0.1	−0.2	−0.2	−0.2	−0.2	20.8	S	18.28	S	MA
57	71	0.67	0.39	0.2	0.19	0.2	−0.1	0.24	−0.2	−0.2	3.98	S	8.44	S	ARMA
58	146	0.93	0.84	0.7	0.6	0.55	0.4	0.41	0.1	0.3	3.52	S	11.08	S	AR
59	53	0.12	−0.2	−0.1	−0.1	−0.2	0.02	−0.3	0	0.18	6.34	S	10.18	S	ARMA
60	66	0.9	0.83	0.75	0.63	0.53	−0.5	−0.5	−0.3	−0.6	3.08	S	8.52	S	AR

Table 4 Autocorrelation coefficients: Day 4

		Lag k									Dickey–Fuller				Class
ID	n	1	2	3	4	5	10	15	20	25	z_t		D_t		
1	61	0.55	0.36	0.2	0.4	0.13	−0.3	−0.1	−0.4	0.05	5.37	S	11.74	S	ARMA
2	84	0.64	0.41	0.13	−0.4	−0.4	−0.5	0.4	−0.4	0.24	6.10	S	13.23	S	AR
3	64	0.64	0.26	0.05	0.16	0.36	0.43	0.1	0	0.17	4.78	S	10.94	S	AR
4	78	0.85	0.7	0.57	0.4	0.31	−0.2	−0.4	−0.5	−0.3	2.82		9.06	S	I
5	252	0.93	0.89	0.85	0.79	0.82	0.68	0.48	0.29	0.09	5.35	S	19.71	S	AR
6	331	0.85	0.69	0.6	0.53	0.41	0.16	0.17	0	0	6.10	S	18.89	S	AR
7	67	0.98	0.95	0.91	0.85	0.78	0.37	−0.2	−0.6	−0.6	1.45		8.42	S	I
8	333	0.91	0.82	0.74	0.68	0.62	0.36	0.24	0.16	0.13	4.42	S	18.93	S	AR
9	55	0.21	0	−0.4	−0.5	−0.1	−0.2	0	−0.4	0	6.60	S	11.47	S	ARMA
11	114	0.56	0.34	0.26	0.17	0.12	−0.2	−0.1	0.02	−0.1	6.43	S	14.90	S	ARMA
12	84	0	0.02	−0.1	0.16	−0.1	0	0.07	0.04	−0.2	9.08	S	15.69	S	MA
15	82	0.97	0.62	0.04	−0.2	−0.3	−0.4	−0.4	−0.4	0.19	4.02	S	8.39	S	AR
16	144	−0.4	−0.1	0.2	0.01	−0.1	−0.1	−0.1	0.13	−0.2	16.2	S	23.73	S	MA
17	175	−0.2	−0.4	−0.3	−0.1	−0.3	−0.3	−0.2	−0.4	−0.2	16.1	S	22.62	S	MA
18	551	0.87	0.76	0.64	0.52	0.42	0.14	0.17	0.12	0.13	7.24	S	26.01	S	AR
19	349	1	1	1	1	1	0.99	0.98	0.98	0.96	3.02	S	16.59	S	I
20	332	0.9	0.8	0.69	0.58	0.43	−0.1	−0.2	0	0.1	6.21	S	21.03	S	AR
21	264	0.86	0.73	0.55	0.37	0.27	0.02	0.18	0.17	−0.1	6.19	S	16.84	S	AR
23	297	0.83	0.74	0.68	0.58	0.5	0.13	−0.2	−0.3	−0.5	5.83	S	20.64	S	AR
24	389	0.94	0.88	0.81	0.72	0.64	0.28	0.02	−0.1	−0.1	3.66	S	17.99	S	AR
25	106	0.88	0.74	0.67	0.57	0.47	−0.1	−0.2	0	0.11	3.25	S	9.81	S	AR
26	472	0.84	0.7	0.56	0.55	0.51	0.2	0.25	0.46	0.37	9.37	S	27.59	S	AR
27	728	0.97	0.95	0.92	0.88	0.83	0.57	0.33	0.24	0.23	4.63	S	26.65	S	AR
29	505	0.82	0.66	0.55	0.5	0.47	0.34	0.26	0.35	0.29	7.79	S	25.13	S	AR
30	648	0.91	0.82	0.74	0.67	0.61	0.37	0.26	0.14	0.03	6.54	S	26.69	S	AR
31	201	0.96	0.92	0.89	0.85	0.82	0.52	0.25	−0.1	−0.1	2.82		15.01	S	I
32	371	0.65	0.43	0.27	0.24	0.22	0.1	0	0.03	0.01	9.50	S	23.40	S	AR
34	718	0.99	0.97	0.96	0.94	0.93	0.85	0.75	0.64	0.53	2.98	S	26.08	S	AR
37	196	0.87	0.74	0.61	0.52	0.44	0.17	−0.2	−0.4	−0.5	4.10	S	14.43	S	AR
38	122	0.73	0.41	0.26	0.28	0.09	0.09	0.14	0.02	0.02	6.02	S	13.56	S	ARMA
39	317	0.98	0.96	0.94	0.91	0.88	0.71	0.56	0.39	0.14	2.45		15.60	S	I
40	269	0.88	0.77	0.66	0.53	0.43	−0.1	−0.3	−0.3	−0.3	5.27	S	16.87	S	AR
41	369	0.99	0.98	0.97	0.95	0.94	0.87	0.73	0.54	0.3	3.25	S	21.16	S	AR
42	162	0.92	0.83	0.73	0.57	0.45	0.08	0	−0.4	−0.4	3.85	S	12.75	S	AR
43	476	0.98	0.96	0.95	0.93	0.91	0.82	0.74	0.66	0.58	2.48		22.17	S	I
45	174	0.93	0.91	0.89	0.9	0.89	0.81	0.75	0.64	0.54	4.47	S	22.21	S	AR
47	121	0.73	0.54	0.48	0.28	0.17	0	0.34	0.27	0	5.01	S	14.17	S	ARMA
48	96	0.95	0.92	0.85	0.77	0.69	0.29	−0.1	−0.2	0.44	1.88		8.09	S	I
49	310	0.95	0.9	0.85	0.79	0.72	0.41	0.19	0.04	−0.1	3.55	S	16.14	S	AR
50	229	0.98	0.93	0.84	0.75	0.65	0.25	0	−0.2	−0.4	2.98	S	12.72	S	AR
52	297	0.96	0.9	0.85	0.79	0.74	0.51	0.13	−0.1	−0.2	3.90	S	16.98	S	AR
53	247	0.96	0.9	0.82	0.72	0.62	0.09	−0.1	−0.1	0.22	4.60	S	16.74	S	AR
56	196	0.44	0.16	0	0.05	0.03	−0.1	0	−0.1	0.01	9.48	S	19.13	S	ARMA
57	96	0.78	0.59	0.38	0.2	0.04	−0.2	−0.2	0.16	0	3.65	S	9.82	S	ARMA
58	184	0.56	0.41	0.18	0.17	−0.1	−0.1	−0.2	0.31	0.22	29	S	17.80	S	AR
60	140	0.68	0.42	0.37	0.3	0.15	−0.2	0	−0.1	0	6.30	S	15.01	S	ARMA

Table 5 Autocorrelation coefficients: Day 5

					Lag k						Dickey–Fuller				Class
ID	n	1	2	3	4	5	10	15	20	25	z_t		D_t		
1	110	0.43	−0.2	0.02	−0.3	−0.2	0.23	−0.2	0.44	−0.4	8.81	S	14.01	S	ARMA
2	117	0.48	0.01	−0.2	0	0	0.5	0.53	0.23	−0.3	9.22	S	16.62	S	ARMA
5	330	0.81	0.65	0.52	0.45	0.39	0.04	−0.1	0.02	0.34	7.77	S	21.27	S	AR
6	473	0.92	0.85	0.76	0.68	0.61	0.44	0.39	0.49	0.47	5.90	S	21.88	S	AR
7	85	85	0.95	0.91	0.84	0.76	0.67	−0.1	−0.4	−0.3	2.40		9.51	S	I
8	271	0.91	0.85	0.8	0.75	0.72	0.48	0.34	0.21	0.09	4.00	S	18.62	S	AR
9	69	69	0.75	0.73	0.69	0.52	0.62	0.68	0.36	−0.2	3.67	S	13.42	S	AR
10	77	77	−0.3	0.68	−0.1	−0.3	−0.1	−0.2	−0.2	−0.3	17.2	S	14.70	S	MA
11	158	0.6	0.42	0.27	0.19	0.26	−0.1	0	0	0.2	6.97	S	17.13	S	ARMA
12	86	86	0.39	0.51	0.4	0.48	0.25	0.3	0.28	0.4	6.26	S	18.06	S	AR
15	133	0.91	0.83	0.81	0.78	0.74	0.67	0.59	0.46	0.47	2.73		12.47	S	I
16	175	−0.4	0.1	−0.1	0.25	0.04	0.09	−0.3	0.07	0.05	18.7	S	28.97	S	MA
17	242	0.91	0.85	0.81	0.77	0.76	0.56	0.55	0	−0.2	7.29	S	21.63	S	AR
18	756	0.95	0.91	0.87	0.82	0.78	0.56	0.46	0.4	0.32	4.96	S	27.34	S	AR
19	357	1	1	1	1	1	1	1	1	1	5.76	S	8.25	S	I
20	395	0.93	0.82	0.68	0.56	0.4	0.03	−0.1	0.03	−0.1	6.13	S	19.73	S	AR
21	348	0.97	0.94	0.92	0.89	0.86	0.75	0.57	0.5	0.38	3.32	S	19.61	S	AR
22	66	66	0.03	0	0.02	−0.2	0	0.13	−0.3	−0.2	2.70	S	12.77	S	AR
23	395	0.86	0.77	0.69	0.65	0.59	0.47	0.53	0.54	0.48	5.89	S	24.12	S	AR
24	325	0.92	0.85	0.76	0.67	0.58	0.18	0	−0.1	−0.1	4.40	S	18.14	S	AR
25	69	69	0.95	0.86	0.68	0.48	0.29	0.06	0.33	−0.3	2.22		7.34	S	I
26	406	0.58	0.39	0.23	0.21	0.18	0.15	−0.1	0.02	0.08	13.1	S	28.99	S	ARMA
27	1149	0.98	0.96	0.94	0.91	0.89	0.76	0.59	0.48	0.36	5.25	S		S	AR
29	182	0.85	0.73	0.65	0.57	0.54	0.31	0.03	−0.1	−0.3	3.94	S	14.93	S	AR
30	977	0.99	0.98	0.98	0.97	0.97	0.94	0.9	0.86	0.82	3.26	S	35.18	S	AR
31	298	0.99	0.97	0.93	0.91	0.9	0.81	0.69	0.51	0.41	2.52		18.46	S	I
32	306	0.62	0.39	0.25	0.09	0	−0.1	0.18	0.02	−0.1	9.44	S	22.69	S	ARMA
33	78	78	0.02	−0.1	0	0.57	−0.2	−0.4	−0.3	−0.4	49.5	S	14.08	S	ARMA
34	608	0.99	1	0.99	0.99	0.99	0.98	0.96	0.95	0.93	2.05		25.36	S	I
37	218	0.88	0.77	0.64	0.57	0.51	0.12	0	−0.1	−0.2	4.50	S	15.31	S	AR
38	136	0.73	0.55	0.33	0.22	0.18	−0.1	0	0.25	0.2	5.44	S	14.80	S	ARMA
39	324	0.97	0.92	0.88	0.84	0.8	0.62	0.47	0.3	0.15	3.56	S	17.09	S	AR
40	341	0.94	0.89	0.81	0.73	0.67	0.41	0.21	0.32	0.3	4.47	S	18.94	S	AR
41	435	1	0.99	0.99	0.98	0.98	0.97	0.97	0.96	0.96	2.04		23.93	S	I
42	123	0.88	0.77	0.71	0.65	0.58	0.21	0.31	0.57	0.31	3.65	S	12.14	S	AR
43	450	0.99	0.98	0.98	0.98	0.97	0.96	0.95	0.92	0.9	2.88		23.86	S	I
44	85	85	0.48	0.3	0.31	0.3	0.32	0.11	−0.1	0.24	5.54	S	13.32	S	AR
45	128	0.36	0.49	0.21	0.3	0.4	0.23	0.05	0.24	0.07	30.6	S	15.38	S	AR
46	97	97	−0.1	−0.4	−0.2	0.54	−0.1	0	0.14	0	10.3	S	14.36	S	MA
47	195	0.73	0.55	0.6	0.5	0.47	0.26	0.3	0.24	0.36	8.22	S	19.83	S	AR
48	130	0.95	0.87	0.79	0.7	0.59	0.39	0.53	0.23	0.07	3.05	S	10.07	S	AR
49	434	0.98	0.98	0.97	0.96	0.95	0.89	0.84	0.8	0.79	2.49		20.97	S	I
50	242	0.96	0.89	0.81	0.71	0.63	0.43	0.21	0.03	−0.1	3.53	S	12.66	S	AR
51	125	0.56	0.38	0.2	0.1	0.19	0.04	0.24	0	0.03	6.71	S	15.38	S	ARMA
52	290	0.89	0.76	0.63	0.57	0.51	0.08	−0.1	−0.1	−0.1	5.18	S	16.77	S	AR
53	300	0.81	0.61	0.43	0.34	0.31	0.21	0.03	−0.1	0.15	7.83	S	20.09	S	AR
55	988	0.83	0.65	0.48	0.35	0.22	0.01	0.03	0.08	−0.2	11.2	S	32.12	S	AR
56	218	0.47	0.09	−0.1	0	0.04	0.1	−0.2	0.1	−0.1	9.77	S	18.62	S	ARMA
57	114	0.88	0.77	0.66	0.55	0.46	0.15	−0.1	−0.1	−0.1	3.04	S	10.71	S	AR
58	288	0.88	0.72	0.6	0.49	0.38	0.21	−0.3	−0.2	0	9.26	S	14.79	S	AR
59	73	73	−0.1	−0.3	0	−0.1	0.17	0.03	−0.1	0.26	9.28	S	13.59	S	MA
60	213	0.35	0.12	0.08	0.09	0.09	0.11	0.1	−0.1	0.16	10.8	S	19.77	S	AR
61	417	0.41	0.14	0.06	0	0.02	−0.1	0.08	0.14	0	13.4	S	26.93	S	AR

Appendix III: Runs test

A run is a sequence of data that exhibit the same characteristics; the sequence is preceded and followed by different data or no data at all ... (Triola and Franklin, 1994, pp. 704–20).

The following hypotheses are tested:

H_0:   The sequence of Buy (B) and Sell (S) decisions of a person-day stream shows no systematic strategy (the sequence is random).

H_a: The sequence of Buy (B) and Sell (S) decisions of a person-day stream shows a systematic strategy (the sequence is not random).

The test statistic for these hypotheses is as follows:

$$Z = \frac{G - \mu_G}{\sigma_G}$$

where the mean number of runs

$$\mu_G = \frac{2n_b n_s}{n_b + n_s} + 1$$

and the standard deviation of the number of runs

$$\sigma_G = \sqrt{\frac{(2n_b n_s)(2n_b n_s - n_b - n_s)}{(n_b + n_s)^2(n_b + n_s - 1)}}$$

and n_b, n_s are the number of Buy (B) or Sell (S) elements in the sequence and G is the number of runs. For example, consider the following partial sequence of buy/sell decisions:

...BBBBssBBBBBBssBBBBBsBBBBBBBssBBBBsBBBBssBBBBBBsBBBBBBsBBBB...
  1   2   3   4   5   6   7   8   9 10 11 12   13   14   15 16   17

In this case, $G = 17$ runs,
$n_b = 46$ (a total of 46 buy decisions)
$n_s = 12$ (a total of 12 sell decisions)

$$\mu_G = \frac{2.46.12}{46 + 12} + 1 = 20.034,$$

and

$$\sigma_G = \sqrt{\frac{(2.46.12)(2.46.12 - 46 - 12)}{(46 + 12)^2(46 + 12 - 1)}} = 2.454,$$

so that test statistic

$$z = \frac{17 - 20.034}{2.454} = -1.236.$$

On this basis, the null hypothesis is accepted at the 5% level.

Endnotes

Chapter 3

1   This importance is further reflected in the psychology literature by research concerned with how decision makers use outcome feedback to learn to improve performance in dynamic decision tasks (for example, Brehmer, 1990, 1992, 1995). A recent study by Gibson *et al* (1997) takes the first steps down the road towards a process theory of learning in dynamic decision tasks.

2   There exists a whole body of literature addressing Samuelson's (1963) theorem that an individual's refusal of a one-off, unique gamble prevents the rational acceptance of multiple plays (repeated) of the same gamble by a SEU maximiser. Lopes (1981, 1996) has long argued against such a claim of irrationality by offering that decision makers may attempt to maximise the probability of coming out ahead rather than maximise SEU (or expected value). Under this decision rule, the acceptance of a repeated gamble that would have been refused if played only once would be deemed rational. Subsequent experimental studies (see, for example, Keren and Wagenaar, 1987, and Keren, 1991) provide evidence that individuals choose differently under unique and repeated conditions.

3   The betweenness property requires that an investor's preference for a given security, which comprises a probability mixture of two other securities, must lie between the investor's preference for the two securities that make up the probability mixture.

4   The separation theorem states that any investor, regardless of their degree of risk aversion, should hold the exact same portfolio of widely diversified shares, the market portfolio. Individuals are able to alter the riskiness of their own portfolios by adjusting their level of lending or borrowing at the risk-free rate of interest. The CAPM is the most widely adopted model of equilibrium asset returns in the finance literature. The model identifies the expected return for a single share, given the risk of holding that share relative to the market portfolio. The exact specification of the CAPM is discussed in more detail in Chapter 5.

5   See MacKinnon (1991).

6   Given the definition of z_t adopted in this chapter, it is apparent that the data in row 4 of Table 3.1 is not included in the analysis of the stochastic nature of individuals' decision processes. This is for the simple reason that the decision to see the next price in the series results in no change in the proportion of an individual's cash converted to shares or shares converted to cash, thus z_t is not strictly defined. It is acknowledged, however, that choosing to see the next price is a decision in itself.

7   Box and Jenkins (1970, p. 33).

Chapter 4

1   For example, see Marsh (1979), Holthausen *et al* (1984) and Mikkelson and Partch (1985).

2   The regression excluded all average points with less than 30 observations of demand for shares at a given price.

3   Although there is evidence of noise at the upper ends of the distributions, there is no evidence that extreme trading behaviour increased as the five days progressed.

4 The data illustrated that the heteroscedasticity was of the form:

$$E(\mu_i)^2 = \sigma^2_{\mu i} = k^2(S)$$

and thus the appropriate transformation of the original model is

$$P = \beta_0 + \beta_1 \overline{S}_p + \mu_s \Rightarrow \frac{P}{\overline{S}_p} = \frac{1}{\overline{S}_p}(\beta_0 + \mu_s) + \beta_1,$$

where $\overline{S}_p$ = Average shares demanded; P = Price and σ^2 = observation variance, etc. (see Judge *et al*, 1985).

5 Part of the explanation for the levels of $\overline{R}^2$s in the unadjusted and truncated regressions is the influence of the slope coefficient on the measurement of $\overline{R}^2$, namely

$$\overline{R}^2 = b_1 \frac{\sum xy}{\sum y^2}.$$

In other words, *ceteris paribus*, the smaller the slope coefficient, the lower the $\overline{R}^2$. The relatively small slope coefficient for day 5 may be one reason for the relatively low $\overline{R}^2$ on day 5. A further issue is the exceptionally high $\overline{R}^2$s for the transformed regressions. These are largely explained by dividing through the whole function by the square root of the independent variable; see endnote 4. The consequence of this for the $\overline{R}^2$s in the present regressions is that the influence of the slope is reduced and the transformed dependent variable is regressed upon a constant term that is largely equivalent to itself. In other words, the fit of the general approach can be better gauged from the untransformed regressions.

Chapter 5

1 The decision data are a series of partially dependent decisions. The portfolio balance and wealth at the beginning of each decision is determined in part by a series of prior decisions. For this reason, we adopted the Kolmogorov–Smirnov test for normality (see Hogg and Tanis, 1988, pp. 591–5), as a suitable non-parametric comparison of the distributions. We are testing $H_0 : R_{\text{portfolio}} = R_{\text{share prices}}$ where the distribution of share price returns is assumed to be normal (discussed below). The test statistic is $D_n = \sup_i[|R_{\text{portfolio}}(i) - R_{\text{share price}}(i)|]$ for n observations.

References

Affleck-Graves, J. and McDonald, B., 1989, Nonnormalities and tests of asset pricing theories, *Journal of Finance*, **44**, 889–908.

Allais, M., 1953, Le comportement de l'homme rationnel devant la risque: critique des postulats et axioms de l'école Américaine, *Econometrica*, **21**, 503–546.

Allais, M. and Hagen, O., 1979, eds, *Expected utility hypothesis and the Allais paradox*, Reidel, Dordrecht.

Andreassen, P.B., 1988, Explaining the price-volume relationship: The difference between price changes and changing prices, *Organizational Behavior and Human Decision Processes*, **41**, 371–389.

Andreassen, P.B. and Kraus, S.J., 1990, Judgmental extrapolation and the salience of change, *Journal of Forecasting*, **9**, 347–372.

Ansic, D., 1995, A pilot experimental test of trade hysteresis, *Managerial and Decision Economics*, **16**(2), 177–183.

Ansic, D. and Keasey, K., 1994, Repeated decisions and attitudes to risk, *Economic Letters*, **45**, 185–189.

Black, F., 1986, Noise, *Journal of Finance*, **41**, 529–543.

Box, G.E.P. and Jenkins, G.M., 1970, *Time series analysis*, Holden Day, San Francisco.

Brehmer, B., 1990, Strategies in real-time, dynamic decision making. In *Insights from Decision Making*, R. Hogarth, ed., University of Chicago Press, Chicago.

Brehmer, B., 1992, Dynamic decision making: Human control of complex systems. *Acta Psychologica*, **81**, 211–241.

Brehmer, B., 1995, Feedback delays in complex dynamic decision tasks. In *Complex problem solving: The European perspective*, P. Frensch and J. Funke, eds, Erlbaum, Hillsdale, NJ.

D'Agostino, R.B. and Pearson, E.S., 1973, Tests for departure from normality: Empirical results for the distributions of b_2 and $\sqrt{b_1}$, *Biometrika*, **60**, 613–622.

Dixit, A., 1989, Hysteresis import penetration, and exchange rate pass through, *Quarterly Journal of Economics*, **104** (2): 205–227.

Elster, J., 1979, *Ulysses and the sirens*, Cambridge University Press, Cambridge.

Evans, D.A., Phillips, M.D. and Holcomb, J.H., 1991, Tests of the betweenness property in experimental financial choices, *Journal of Economic Behavior and Organisations*, **15**, 279–295.

Fama, E.F., 1965, The behaviour of stock market prices, *Journal of Business*, **38**, 34–105.

Friedman, M., 1953, The methodology of positive economics. In *The methodology of positive economics*, pp. 3–43, University of Chicago, Chicago.

Friedman, D. and Rust, J., 1993, *The double auction market: Institutions, theories and evidence*, Addison Wesley, Reading.

Friedman, D. and Sunder, S., (1994) *Experimental methods: A primer for economists*, Cambridge University Press, Cambridge.

Gans, J.S., (1996) On the impossibility of rational choice under incomplete information, *Journal of Economic Behaviour and Organisation*, **29**, 287–309.

Gibson, F.P., Fichman, M. and Plaut, D.C., 1997, Learning in dynamic decision tasks: Computational model and empirical performance, *Organizational Behavior and Human Decision Processes*, **71**, 1–35.

Gujarati, D.N., 1995, *Basic econometrics*, 3rd ed., McGraw-Hill, New York.

Hey, J.D., 1983, Whither uncertainty?, *Economic Journal*, Supplement, 130–139.

Hey, J.D., 1991, *Experiments in economics*, Blackwell, Oxford.

Hey, J.D., 1992, Experiments in economics—and psychology. In *New directions in economic psychology: Theory, experiment and application*, S.E.G. Lea, P. Webley and B.M. Young, eds., Edward Elgar, Brighton.

Hogg, V.R. and Tanis, E.A., 1988, *Probability and statistical inference*, 3rd ed., Macmillan, New York.

Holthausen, R., Leftwich, R. and Mayers, D., 1984, The effect of large block trades: A cross-sectional analysis, unpublished manuscript, The University of Chicago, Chicago.

Hudson, R., Keasey, K., Littler, K. and Dempsey, M., 1997, Time diversification: An essay in the need to revisit finance theory, *Centre for Financial Services Working Paper*, The University of Leeds, Leeds.

Joan, S.G., Mowen, J.C. and Gentry, J.W., 1990, Risk perception in a simulated industrial purchasing task: The effects of single versus multi-play decisions, *Journal of Behavioral Decision Making*, **3**, 91–108

Judge, G.G., Griffiths, W.E., Hill, R.C., Lutkepohl, H. and Lee, T.C., 1985, *The theory and practice of econometrics*, 2nd ed., Wiley, New York.

Keasey, K. and Moon, P., 1996, Gambling with the house money in capital expenditure decisions: An experimental analysis, *Economic Letters*, **50**, 105–110.

Keren, G., 1991, Additional tests of utility theory under unique and repeated conditions, *Journal of Behavioral Decision Making*, **4**, 297–304.

Keren, G. and Wagenaar, W.A., 1987, Violation of utility theory in unique and repeated gambles, *Journal of Experimental Psychology: Learning, Memory and Cognition*, **13**, 387–391.

Keynes, J.M., 1961, *A general theory of employment, interest and money*, 13th ed., Macmillan, London.

Kim, Y.C., 1973, Choice in the lottery insurance situation: Augmented income approach, *Quarterly Journal of Economics*, **87**, 148–156.

Kroll, Y., Levy, H. and Rapaport, A., 1988a, Experimental tests of the separation theorem and the capital asset pricing model, *The American Economic Review*, **78**, 500–519.

Kroll, Y., Levy, H. and Rapaport, A., 1988b, Experimental tests of the mean-variance model for portfolio selection, *Organizational Behavior and Human Decision Processes*, **42**, 388–410.

Krugman, P., 1989, *Exchange rate instability*, The MIT Press, Cambridge.

Loomes, G. and Sugden, R., 1982, Regret theory: An alternative theory of rational choice under uncertainty, *Economic Journal*, **92**, 805–824.

Loomes, G. and Sugden, R., 1983, Regret theory and measurable utility, *Economics Letters*, **12**, 19–21.

Lopes, L.L., 1981, Decision making in the short run, *Journal of Experimental Psychology: Learning, Memory and Cognition*, **7**, 377–385.

Lopes, L.L., 1996, When time is of the essence: Averaging, aspiration and the short run, *Organizational Behavior and Human Decision Processes*, **65**, 179–189.

Lumby, S., 1991, *Investment appraisal and financing decisions*, 4th ed., Chapman and Hall, London.

Machina, M.J., 1987, Decision making in the presence of risk, *Science*, **236**, 537–543.

MacKinnon, J.G., 1991, Critical values of cointegration tests. In R.F. Engle and C.W.J. Granger, eds., *Long run economic relationships: Readings in cointegration*, Chapter 13, Oxford University Press, New York.

Mandelbrot, B., 1963, Variation of speculative prices, *Journal of Business*, **36**, 394–419.

Marsh, P., 1979, Equity rights issues and the efficiency of the UK stock market, *The Journal of Finance*, **34**(4), 820–862.

McCardle, K.F. and Winkler, R.L., 1992, Repeated gambles, learning and risk aversion, *Management Science*, **38**, 807–818.

Mikkelson, W.H. and Partch, M.M., 1985, Stock price effects on secondary distributions, *Journal of Financial Economics*, **14**, June, 165–194.

Pearson, E.S., D'Agostino, R.B. and Bowman, K.O., 1977, Tests for departure from normality, *Biometrika*, **64**, 231–246.

Plott, C. R. and Sunder, S., 1982, Efficiency of experimental security markets with insider information: An application of rational-expectations models, *Journal of Political Economy*, **90**, 663–698.

Plott, C. R. and Sunder S., 1988, Rational expectations and the aggregation of diverse information in laboratory security markets, *Econometrica*, **56**, 1085–1118.

Reichenstein, W. and Dorsett, D., 1995, *Time diversification revisited*, The Research Foundation of the Institute of Chartered Financial Analysts, Charlottesville.

Richardson, M. and Smith, T., 1993, A test for multivariate normality in stock returns, *Journal of Business*, **66**, 295–321.

Roth, A.E., 1990, *Laboratory experiments in economics: Six points of view*, Cambridge University Press, Cambridge.

Samuelson, P.A., 1963, Risk and uncertainty: A fallacy of large numbers, *Scientia*, **98**, 108–113.

Savage, L.J., 1972, *The foundations of statistics*, 2nd ed., Dover, New York.

Shefrin, H. and Statman, M., 1985, The disposition to sell winners too early and ride losers too long: Theory and evidence, *The Journal of Finance*, **XL**, 777–792.

Shleifer, A., 1986, Do demand curves for stocks slope down?, *The Journal of Finance*, **3**, June, 579–590.

Smith, V.L., 1982, Theory, experiment and economics. Reproduced in Smith, V.L., 1991, *Papers in experimental economics*, Cambridge University Press, New York.

Smith, V.L., 1991, *Papers in experimental economics*, Cambridge University Press, New York.

Smith, V.L., 1994, Economics in the laboratory, *Journal of Economic Perspectives*, **8**, 113–131.

Stout, L.A., 1990, Are takeover premiums really premiums? Market price, fair value and corporate law, *Yale Law Journal*, **99**, 1235–1296.

Sunder, S., 1995, Experimental asset markets: A survey. In J. H. Kagel and A.E. Roth, eds., *The handbook of experimental economics*, Chapter 6, Princeton University Press, Princeton.

Thaler, R.H. and Johnson, E.J., 1990, Gambling with the house money and trying to break even: The effects of prior outcomes on risky choices, *Management Science*, **36**, 643–660.

Triola, M.F. and Franklin, L.R., 1994, *Business statistics*, Addison-Wesley, Reading, Mass.

Tversky, A. and Kahneman, D., 1981, The framing of decisions and the psychology of choice, *Science*, **211**, 453–458.

Von Neuman, J. and Morgenstern, O., 1947, *Theory of games and economic behavior*, 2nd ed., Princeton University Press, Princeton.

Wedell, D.H. and Bockenholt, U., 1990, Moderation of preference reversals in the long run, *Journal of Experimental Psychology: Human Perception and Performance*, **16**, 429–438.

Wilde, L., 1980, On the use of laboratory experiments in economics. In *The philosophy of economics*, J. Pitt, ed., Reidel, Dordrecht.